Sorrow of
the Earth

ÉRIC VUILLARD

Sorrow of the Earth

Buffalo Bill, Sitting Bull
and the Tragedy of Show Business

Translated from the French
by Ann Jefferson

PUSHKIN PRESS
LONDON

Pushkin Press
71–75 Shelton Street
London WC2H 9JQ

Original text © Actes Sud, 2014
Translation © Ann Jefferson, 2016

First published in French as *Tristesse de la terre* in 2014
This translation first published by Pushkin Press in 2016

INSTITUT
FRANÇAIS

This book is supported by the Institut français
(Royaume-Uni) as part of the Burgess Programme

1 3 5 7 9 8 6 4 2

ISBN 978 1 782272 21 2

Set in Paperback by Tetragon, London
Printed in Great Britain by the CPI Group, UK

www.pushkinpress.com

to Stéphane Tiné
and Pierre Bravo Gala

CONTENTS

The Museum of Mankind   9

What Is the Essence of Spectacle?   15

An Actor   23

Buffalo Bill in Alsace-Lorraine   35

The Massacre of Wounded Knee   49

Buying a Child   61

The "Battle" of Wounded Knee   75

The Town of Cody   97

Reality Isn't What It Used to Be   113

The Princes of
Entertainment Die in Sorrow   123

Histories   135

Snow   143

The Museum
of Mankind

SPECTACLE IS THE ORIGIN OF THE WORLD.
Tragedy stands before us, motionless and strangely
anachronistic. And so, in Chicago, at the World's
Columbian Exposition of 1893 commemorating the
400th anniversary of Columbus's voyage, a display of
relics on a stall in the central aisle included the desiccated corpse of a newborn Indian baby. There were
twenty-one million visitors. They promenaded on the
wooden balconies of the Idaho Building, admired
the miracles of technology, like the gigantic choco-
late Venus de Milo at the entrance to the agricul-
tural pavilion, and then bought cones of sausages
for ten cents apiece. Huge numbers of buildings had
been erected, and the place resembled a gimcrack
St Petersburg, with its arches, its obelisks, its plaster
architecture borrowed from every age and every land.
The black-and-white photographs we have convey
the illusion of an extraordinary city, with palaces

fringed by statues and fountains, and ornamental pools down to which stone steps slowly descend. Yet it's all fake.

But the highlight of the Columbian Exposition, its apotheosis, the feature that was to attract the greatest number of spectators, was the Wild West Show. Everyone wanted to see it. And Charles Bristol—the proprietor of the stall with the Indian relics and the exhibit of the baby's corpse—also wanted to drop everything and go! He already knew the spectacle, because right at the start of his career, he had been the manager and wardrobe master for the Wild West Show. But it was no longer the same, and it had now become a colossal enterprise. There were two performances a day, and eighteen thousand seats. Horses galloped past a backdrop of gigantic painted canvases. It wasn't the loose string of rodeos and sharpshooters that he had known, but a veritable enactment of History. So while the Columbian Exposition was celebrating the industrial revolution, Buffalo Bill was glorifying conquest.

Later on, much later on, Charles Bristol had worked for the Kickapoo Indian Medicine Company, which employed nearly eight hundred Indians and around fifty Whites to sell its stuff. Its flagship medicine was Sagwa, a mixture of herbs and alcohol for the treatment of rheumatism and dyspepsia. And it would appear that cowboys suffered particularly from wind and borborygmic dyspepsia, because right across the country people were in search of a remedy. Eventually, Charles Bristol abandoned the sale of medicines and embarked on a series of long tours with his collection of *objets d'art*. Two Winnebago Indians who were part of the Medicine Company had decided to follow him. The museum toured in the Midwest and the little sketches it staged, where the Indians performed dances to illustrate the specific function of each object, were both entertaining and educational.

Towards the end of 1890, barely three years before the Columbian Exposition, Charles Bristol had joined forces with a bum by the name of Riley Miller. Once Bristol chummed up with Riley, the story becomes hard to credit. Previously, according to him, Bristol had accumulated his treasures thanks to his Indian friendships—a long succession of little gifts. But Riley Miller was a murderer and a thief. He would scalp and strip dead Indians: he murdered them and then took their moccasins, their weapons, their shirts, their hair—everything. Men, women or children. A part of the relics displayed by Bristol at the Chicago Fair came from these activities. Later on, the history museum in Nebraska bought Charles Bristol's collection; and today, somewhere in the museum's reserve collection, you might well come across the desiccated body of the Indian baby from the Exposition. What this tells us is that show business and the human sciences had their origins in the same displays, with curiosities lifted from the dead. Which means that today, what you find on museum shelves throughout the world is nothing but trophies and plunder. And all the African, Indian or Asian objects that we admire were stolen off corpses.

What Is the Essence of Spectacle?

LET US GO BACK A LITTLE, to a time a few years before the Chicago Columbian Exposition, and take a closer look at the tremendous Wild West Show. What force of attraction can bring forty thousand people a day to see this spectacle? Down what incline in their fleeting lives do they slide to reach the great arena where yelling horsemen gallop through cardboard scenery? It was ten years before the Great Exposition that Buffalo Bill set up his show; the thing was none-theless put together gradually, incorporating new acts, piecemeal fashion, one after the other. The early version was most likely nothing more than a tedious succession of rodeos, but Buffalo Bill didn't stop there. When the former scout took to the stage, he was determined to revolutionize the art of entertainment and make it into *something different.* So Buffalo Bill dragged his circus from town to town, improving the acts and recruiting new stars; but as it developed, the Wild West Show acquired a new form of success; it was no longer just a circus, no longer a troupe of acrobats performing on stage. No, it was something quite new. And yet, when you looked carefully, it was all rather ramshackle, just a string of little numbers; and there was nothing very extraordinary about it, no monsters, no hideous creatures; so what was it, then?

Movement and action. Reality itself. Yes, just galloping horses, re-enacted battles, suspense, people falling down dead and getting up again. It had everything. And the audiences grew all the time, clapping, laughing, shouting, enthralled, completely spellbound; as if the world had been created in a drum roll.

However, the real spark was elsewhere. The central idea of the Wild West Show lay somewhere else. The aim was to astound the public with an intimation of suffering and death which would never lose its grip on them. They had to be drawn out of themselves, like little silver fish in a landing net. They had to be presented with human figures who shriek and collapse in a pool of blood. There had to be consternation and terror, hope, and a sort of clarity, an extreme truth cast across the whole of life. Yes, people had to shudder—a spectacle must send a shiver through everything we know, it must catapult us ahead of ourselves, it must strip us of our certainties and sear us. Yes, a spectacle sears us, despite what its detractors say. A spectacle steals from us, and lies to us, and intoxicates us, and gives us the world in every shape and form. And sometimes, the stage seems to exist *more* than the world, it is more present than our own lives, more moving and more persuasive than reality, more terrifying than our nightmares.

And in order to bring in an audience, in order to get ever more people wanting to come and see the Wild West Show, they had to be told a story, the story that millions of Americans, and then millions of Europeans, wanted to hear, the only story they wanted to hear, and the one that, perhaps without knowing it, they were already hearing in the crackle of the electric light bulbs. The inhabitants of American cities, this new breed of humans whose disquiet is a stubborn question addressed only to them, and to no one else, who in the depths of their angst have a sense of being set apart, designated by the spirit of progress to seize the torch of humanity and hold it higher than anyone has ever held it before, let me tell you, these inhabitants of the cities of America wanted to witness something different, they wanted to travel across the Great Plains in their imagination, to ride through the canyons of Colorado and experience the lives of the pioneers. It might appear strange, but by means of the lives of the pioneers and the turbulent tales of their migration, the inhabitants of the young American cities wanted to be present at a live broadcast of their own History, that great display of courage and violence which, a few thousand miles away, was still in the making.

All this was very splendid, but in reality, thanks to a fetid emanation from the crowd or an effluence from the soul, Buffalo Bill knew that it wasn't the cowpokes or the sharpshooters that the crowds came to see. No. The power of his spectacle (and he probably didn't really know where it came from), the idea that gave it its authentic substance, the thing that made it irresistible was the presence of the Indians, real Indians. Yes, that was the only thing that people came for. Oh! of course they didn't realize this themselves, because most of them despised Indians. But if they scrimped and saved to buy tickets for every member of the family, and took their seats quietly in a row on the bleachers, it was unquestionably to see the Indians and not for any other reason. So Buffalo Bill had to show Indians. And for such a spectacle to prosper, he had to keep coming up with new stars.

For this, apart from Buffalo Bill himself, there was Major John Burke, his impresario. Like most of the people who wore cuffs in those days, John Burke wasn't a major at all. You come across him sometimes under the name of Arizona John, although he had never been to Arizona either. He was just a swindler of the worst kind. In those days, any nincompoop could found a city, become a general, a businessman, a governor or President of the United States; and perhaps this is still the case. John Burke had sensed the coming of the vast machinery of a culture of spectacle, and was now press officer to Buffalo Bill—his publicity agent. He was the greatest and the wackiest publicity agent. Thanks to a perfect match between the man and his times, the former journalist, broker and one-time leader of a troupe of acrobats became the inventor of show business.

An Actor

CIVILIZATION IS A HUGE and insatiable beast. It feeds on everything. It needs pepper, and tea, and coal, and tin. It is impossible ever to satisfy. Civilization also demands less material sustenance, but it quickly wearies of its fare. It constantly requires new recruits, new faces. And so the Wild West Show had regularly to hire more actors. And for this, there is something better than artistes, better than the best acrobats, better than any freak of nature. There are the real protagonists of History. Just think about it! You can always pay a juggler to astound an audience, you can always dig out a hunchback or a pair of Siamese twins to draw a curious crowd. But getting tens of thousands of people to come every day, to make fifteen thousand, twenty thousand people pay over a dollar, morning and evening for years on end, requires something more than jugglers and hunchbacks. It requires something quite unprecedented.

And this was why, one morning in 1885, after several years of exile and imprisonment, the old Indian chief Sitting Bull, victor at the Battle of the Little Big Horn, received a visit from John Burke.

The big beast had come alone. The weather was glorious. As he perched on his sprung phaeton, between two jolts of his vehicle, John Burke had carefully pondered his plan. It's true that the road bucked a little too much for a man of his girth, the potholes and the humpback bridges had caused him a fair degree of misery. He had driven grumbling alongside a never-ending avenue of willows, then taken a narrow track that cut across a boundless plain. But although he was much tried by his journey, once he arrived, his manner was relaxed and affable. Yes, he'd come with a mouth full of pieties, a few small presents and a clear blue sky. He offered a cigar to the Indian, who refused it. He smoked his nabob's peace pipe by himself, before the silent Indian. After the usual exchange of greetings, during which a sly and ferocious battle was instantly engaged, John Burke launched into a long, convoluted, labyrinthine and meandering speech. Between two compliments he rearranged his hair, pushing it back and clamping it round his ears. But the old Indian maintained an obstinate silence. And after a quarter of an hour of chatter, John Burke realized that his hedging about was getting him nowhere; Sitting Bull seemed cagey, and he would do better to get to the point.

The Indian chief had long since known that the white man presented constantly changing faces and that he should not be taken in by any of them; they were all after something. To the panoply of those he already knew—trappers, soldiers, pioneers, cowboys, liquor sellers—he was now about to add that of impresario. But Sitting Bull already had a little showbiz experience; the previous year he had been exhibited among the waxwork figures of a museum in New York. Once the flood of weasel words dried up, he negotiated fifty dollars a week, plus an advance, all expenses to be covered by the impresario, and above all, in a codicil that he insisted on adding: he would retain exclusive rights over the sale of photographs of himself along with the use of his autograph. John Burke didn't prolong the negotiations, because Sitting Bull was a choice attraction for the Wild West Show. So the contract was signed, and the Indian chief joined the troupe.

His first performance was a photographic pose. Sitting Bull and Buffalo Bill were escorted to a small booth where, with their feet on a carpet of straw, they had to stand in front of an emaciated birch tree daubed onto a canvas that supposedly depicted the untamed West. Sitting Bull looks somewhat ill at ease in this decor, like a misplaced remnant of the Creation.

Suddenly no one moves, or barely, and for a few moments, during the morsel of time needed for the tiny motes of light to settle on the large chemical plate, Sitting Bull and Buffalo Bill shake hands. The photographer disappears behind his theatre curtain, and Sitting Bull feels a profound solitude which thrusts him into that cold, godforsaken place where we stand rigid for as long as our relics last. In that moment, he forgets everything. He even forgets his dead brothers. The tepees, the fields, the encampments, the long journeys, he forgets it all. The river bears away his memories in a roar of foam. But as the light shines through the clump of trees, it's not just his stiff torso, his hardened, spare profile that is petrified like a great vessel of nostalgia. It's as if there were something awaiting him in the photograph. He stands, at point-blank range, in the confusion of his selfhood, before the tiny leather accordion and the photographer's black hood. Hold it! The bulb is raised, a hand squeezes. Through the small hole his soul looks out at him. Pop! It's done. The silhouettes of the old Indian and Buffalo Bill hover for a few moments on the gelatine, amid the silver atoms. And then they're fixed for evermore on sheets of tickertape measuring seventeen centimetres by twelve. In this famous photograph, Sitting Bull and Buffalo Bill hold each other by the hand for all eternity. However, not only does this handshake mean nothing—it's just a publicity stunt—but if it's to be any use in the advertising campaign, the photo has to contain two contradictory messages: both the reconciliation between two peoples and the moral and physical superiority of the Americans. Which is why in the photograph Buffalo Bill exaggeratedly puffs out his chest in an attempt to give himself a more dignified air. He stands very straight, his left leg thrust slightly forward, his head held regally high, sizing up the Indian. Sitting Bull stares into the void, and simply extends his hand. Progress wins out. We look on with perplexity.

*

I don't know exactly where in the United States Sitting Bull made his first stage appearance and began his acting career; but the show never changed very much. Right at the beginning, while "The Star-Spangled Banner" is being intoned, Buffalo Bill suddenly appears: he's on horseback, his arm is raised, and he holds his hat in his hand. Cowboys and Indians parade around him, also on horseback. A trumpet sounds. And then, the person everyone has been waiting for enters the arena. For the highlight of the show isn't a show, it's reality. Yes, there's nothing to beat it! Reality is an excessive thing; it's everywhere and nowhere; and for some time now it seems to have been fading. It's strange, and it's hard to explain: reality is still there but it's as if it had lost its substance. Everything you thought it was founded on has suddenly been disrupted, altered, damaged, exposed. Nothing looks the same; everything seems to have been swept up by speed, money and trade! And you can't really say what former dreams and images fill you with regret. What do we regret? What society? What ideal? What sweetness?

And now the show is starting. An Indian enters the arena; it's the victor of the Battle of the Little

Big Horn. He's wearing his finest costume. "Ladies and gentlemen, let me introduce the great Indian chief..." vociferates Frank Richmond from his rostrum.

Sitting Bull has probably never been as alone as he is at this moment, in the midst of the American flags and the great entertainment machine. He wasn't as alone as this when he was living in exile in Canada, with a bunch of other undesirables; the initial darkness is impenetrable. And to be sure, you would be alone on horseback, in the icy rain, wandering between indistinct shapes in the great forest. Yes, you would be alone and sad, but you were free, and you were filled with a burning hatred. And now Sitting Bull is alone in the arena; the grand thing that he loved has been left behind, a long way behind. And here, on the bleachers, this is what people have come for; they've all come to see this, and only this: his solitude.

Previously, no American or any Westerner in the world had ever seen anything. Up until now, all they had seen was their dreams. Yes, until now, from the distant depths of History, they had heard only of Jugurtha and his Numidians, Arabs on horseback,

Chinamen with excessively long plaits, distant enemies. But now the crystal ball has exploded, and the future has vanished in a cloud of dust. The old fable has ended. The first episode of the soap opera is beginning, the season of our triumphs. The veil is rent, the robe is in flames. In the time it takes to count to one, we shall be masters of the world.

This is when the booing and the catcalls start to fly. Sitting Bull remains impassive, he does his lap of the arena. Not for one moment did anyone think to get him to perform an episode from the Indian wars or from some other time his life: a simple parade would suffice. There is no scope for History. The past is surrounded by bleachers, and the spectators want to see its ghosts. But nothing else. They don't want to hear them. They don't want to talk to them. They just want to see them. They want to draw back the curtain for a moment and see the Indian.

And what do we see? What do we hear? What lie is being spelled out in that cadaverous mouth? What is this voice that speaks? What are these false words that dictate our feelings? They seem to come from somewhere deep down, from the very bowels of the

half-formed creatures that we are. We listen distract-
edly, and we allow ourselves be carried along help-
lessly towards the precipice.

The crowd roars and shouts abuse at him. The
people spit. There it is, the unprecedented thing,
the Red Indian we came to see, the strange beast
that prowled around our farmsteads, or so they say.
"That's him!" From the wings Buffalo Bill signs to
Frank Richmond who tries to quiet the spectators.
But it's no use, the Indian chief will have to complete
his lap under the hail of abuse, until he reaches the
end. The hubbub is extraordinary. The journalists
take photographs. Children stare wide-eyed. And
Sitting Bull slowly leaves the arena.

Buffalo Bill in Alsace-Lorraine

SO WHO WAS BUFFALO BILL, the creator and star presenter of the Wild West Show? It's said that he had the build of a lumberjack and the hands of an artist, very delicate hands that were almost too fine, which—as we are informed by the mysteries of science—indicates a predisposition to insanity. And indeed, throughout his life Buffalo Bill would have moments of deep despair, bouts of serious depression. Although he raked in pot-loads of dollars and salvos of applause, as soon as the curtain fell he would find himself alone once more. And no sooner had he removed his make-up in his old entertainer's lair, than he felt a horrible anguish. In front of the mirror, while he mechanically combed his hair after removing his Stetson for the thousandth time, he would feel a terrible pang in the chest—as if his entire being was a void.

At that time, Buffalo Bill's body was already a pure product of marketing, a sort of sham. Nobody knows what lay behind the orgy of publicity. And it's even harder to know what the showbiz entrepreneur, the superstar he had become actually thought about. Yet he wasn't one of those people who leave no trace; but excess is a different kind of problem from insufficiency, and if archaeology is the science of remains, there exists no branch of research devoted to things that have been *exposed too much to sight*. The strangest part of the whole business is the most banal. Buffalo Bill performed the same meaningless scenes over and over again, sticking to the same routines, with the same gusto. Success is a form of vertigo. Repetition must have some reassuring property, some power of hypnosis or truth. As the hero of numerous fanzines, whose existence he was initially unaware of, his life was fashioned by others. He decided neither his name nor his story. Around 1867, when he was working for the railways, the labourers gave him the nickname of Buffalo Bill. Then, by pure chance, between two shots of liquor, he told the tale of his adventures to Ned Buntline who made a dime novel out of them. And the hoodlum's yarn, all blarney, asseveration and fabrication designed to earn him another drink, had become the stuff of serialized fiction. And as one episode followed another, the character of Buffalo Bill, a mix of a night's bragging and the numerous extensions, suffixes and increments added by Buntline with every page, had acquired a sort of celebrity. Later on, Buffalo Bill would learn that an actor, Jason Ward, was playing the part of himself on the stage and that his character had become famous. So nothing had been decided by him. His life escapes him. A great counterfeiting force had sucked him in, replicated him and produced a revised version. In the end, he was induced to play the part of himself. This is how he came to mount the boards, wearing fancy dress, simply to match his own character. He's an imitation of himself. He gradually became the person he was portraying. His life would become a sort of parody of his life, an alternative, fabricated life, pledged to others. The illusion was so powerful, the public so thoroughly won over, that the actors in the show, who had never set foot in the West and never fired anything but blanks, apparently ended up believing the hogwash they narrated, and the adventures they mimed. And so it's said that at the end of his life, after performing the Battle of Little Big Horn dozens of times over, Buffalo Bill genuinely believed that he had taken part in it. To meet the requirements of the show, they had even gone so far as to change the outcome, because audiences prefer a happy ending. Which is how, after years spent successfully perform-ing this amended version of grand History, Buffalo Bill was convinced that he had saved Custer!

But real life is still there. It returns to us with each drop of rain, in the fragile mystery of things. I imag-ine, sleeping in all kinds of hotels, or in his special train, with its saloon, its billiard table, kitchens and bathrooms, Buffalo Bill will be sipping a drink, as large clouds darken his carriage. For a moment, he leans out of the window, and senses the huge locomo-tive, way out in front, very tall and completely black. As the wind slaps his face, he hears the frightful rumbling of the engine. Turning his head, he sees broad, uncultivated expanses, yellow grasses, the remains of a forest bristling with dead pines. He sits down again, his eyes roasted by the smoke. He thinks about all the people who come and go, the people he hires and then fires, as if he were dipping his hand in and out of a bag of salt. And while his fingers hover among the crumbs on the table, amid the worries of the entrepreneur, the last-minute problems he has not yet solved, there rises an obscure sense of remorse.

His temperature had risen. Louisa had sat up all night. It had begun with stomach pains; and after starting off by crying a little, he'd just said where it hurt, and moaned. They'd given him warm water to drink, sat him up in his little bed, and he'd begun to vomit. Then they'd got very scared and sent for the doctor. Buffalo Bill was on tour, far away from home in North Place. Louisa must have felt very alone. This is what he would think about sometimes in his dressing room. He would picture the huge legs of the actress he'd invited up to his bedroom that evening; but could he have known that his son was ill? And what difference would it have made? In the lightning flash of a thought, the face of little Kit would pierce the darkness where all our thoughts live and die, and he felt terribly sad and anxious. Then a moment later, it would be Josepha, the actress, whose name came back to him, and the way he'd sat kneading her breasts, while she panted and thrust her tongue in his mouth and made him come.

And then he would go on drinking, the breach had been opened up, he was thirsty, lost in his eternity. Suddenly, he would think about Louisa when she was very young. How pretty and delicate she was! He thought back to the young woman he had loved and he wondered what had happened to them. He would wonder what had slowly turned the pretty girl from Saint Louis, with her gentle, graceful ways, into this sad, hard woman. Yes, between two performances of the show, when he got up from his little siesta in the afternoon, tired, his face crumpled by sleep and temporarily slashed by the creases in his pillow, in the strange gloom that greets you when you wake in the middle of the day, he would doubtless think about the little boy. Kit Carson Cody, his son, bore the name of a famous scout, as if life and adventure would, for him, always be one and the same. And then he would hear his little voice. For voices remain inside us longer than the rest. Oh! if only I had been there! he would lament, and then he would resume the bitter refrain against his wife, the *mauvaise foi* of the father and the drunk.

He had gone on travelling, burning himself up with his success, taking the glad tidings to the four corners of America. He had been all over the world, to Paris, to London, and even as far as Rome. And finally, after dragging his grief and his fame to the far ends of the earth, outside the Colosseum, where Nero tortured the Christian martyrs, Buffalo Bill requested permission to put on his show. His request was refused. By an irony of fate, the Colosseum wasn't big enough.

And so it was, that going from one railway station to the next, long after Italy, and long after countless other performances, the troupe, which had crossed the Atlantic and travelled round Europe, arrived one fine day in Nancy. The ocean crossing had required several ships. Their hulls contained 1,200 stakes, 4,000 poles, 30,000 metres of rope, 23,000 metres of canvas, 8,000 seats and 10,000 items of wood and iron, all destined to create a hundred big tops lit by three dynamos and crowned by flags from all over the world. The troupe numbered 800 individuals, 500 saddle horses and dozens of bison. It was like another Noah's Ark. The bison swayed in their stalls to the rhythm of the swell and puked into their mangers; they suffered from seasickness.

The troupe finally set everything up at the far end of the boulevard, alongside a country lane. The tents and the bleachers were erected in a few hours. The team was well practised. Buffalo Bill decided to lay on two performances a day, one at two o'clock and the other at eight. Ah! for one franc sixty-five, how happy the youngsters of Nancy and Bar-le-Duc must have been! How enthralled by the bison, those unknown aurochs they'd only ever seen as drawings in the *Larousse* encyclopaedia. People took the tram home from Jarville to the Place Carnot, and then dispersed down the winter streets. It was nearly Christmas, the shop windows were lit, the chestnut sellers bawled their wares, it smelled good, people allowed themselves a moment's reverie, and they bought a few postcards for the grandparents. They'd seen Annie Oakley firing a rifle and smashing hundreds of glass balls to smithereens like a cloud in a dream; and it seemed to them like the dream itself.

Generally, Buffalo Bill gave orders for the camp to be dismantled immediately after the last show. It would be done in less than an hour, like packing up a market stall; and then they would leave without delay for the next stop. But in Nancy, he had learned that there were some worrying disturbances in South Dakota. According to reports, the Indians were rebelling.

He doubtless assembled everyone who worked for him and gave them all kinds of instructions; and after negotiations that he seemed in a hurry to conclude, he rented a small chateau where the troupe could wait it out. Then, as soon as he had issued a few more orders and organized their stay, Buffalo Bill immediately headed for London and returned to the United States as fast as he could. The troupe remained behind in Alsace for several months, alone, with nothing to do. Small parties of anthropologists had plenty of time to measure the skulls of the Indians with a curious sort of compass and to agree a price for their fancy handicrafts with a view to a future museum. And it must have been another spectacle, stranger perhaps than the great spectacular, to see groups of cowboys outside the chateau in Benfeld near Strasbourg, wandering about between the old pond and the farmstead in Muhlbach. And it must have been something else to get an eyeful, from the main road, of a small herd of bison on the edge of the Schiffloch forest. And for several months, the bemused hikers of Alsace would catch sight of the Sioux—driven by boredom out of the camp and into the town—staggering dead drunk down the Rue de la Digue, and then drinking water from the canal.

It's said that in Marseilles, at some point on this tour, an Indian by the name of Feather Man had taken a bad fall. Stuntmen are prone to this kind of mishap. He had been transported to the Hôpital de la Conception. His condition worsened, and the troupe had to move on. So he remained, all alone, on the other side of the world, unable to speak either French or English, in the grip of fever and pain. On 6th January, at four o'clock in the morning, he died after a long, solitary and painful agony. His body was taken to the Saint-Pierre cemetery, where he was buried in section no. 8, trench no. 19, plot no. 2. The years passed. No one claimed the body. His remains were disinterred and thrown into a communal grave.

In every cemetery there's a section set aside for the poor: a small, badly maintained plot, covered by a heavy trapdoor, with no cross, no names, no nothing. Sometimes a pebble is left on the ground, a dried bunch of flowers, a name chalked onto the dirt, a date. And that's all. There is nothing more moving than these graves. They may be the graves of humanity. We owe them a great deal of love.

The Massacre of
Wounded Knee

THE WORLD'S LAST PILGRIMS will be wretched groups of individuals, peoples driven from their lands, men and women who have been deported or cast aside. Long lines of dead people. And so, in Dakota, after a fierce campaign by the ranchers—who spread rumours about an Indian rebellion—tension had palpably risen, and many Indians were planning to flee. The big stockbreeders were hoping to frighten off the farmers who were settling the area in ever greater numbers and whose land was breaking up their vast grazing grounds. They rapidly armed a home guard and set about harassing the Indians. Following a deadly ambush, which killed dozens of warriors, tension rose again and General Nelson Miles ordered the arrest of Sitting Bull.

After one season with the Wild West Show, the Indian chief had abandoned his acting career and returned to live among his own people in the Grand

River reserve. He was old now, and weary. And he wanted to end his days here, in peace.

In the early hours of 15th December 1890, some forty Indian policemen advanced at a trot to within a kilometre or so of Sitting Bull's camp, and then burst into the village at a gallop. Everyone was asleep. Ah! how we love the early morning, the cool air, the great shafts of light on the earth's stony surface. But that morning, it wasn't birds singing, it wasn't a young girl humming as she got dressed in the hut next door, it was the hooves of forty-three horses that the drowsing villagers heard. Profit and the respect for power were responding to the voice of God. History is dead. Scum is all that's left. There's no mistaking the sound of iniquity on the move. General Miles is a creator of examples, a technician of discipline. It's daybreak. We're outside the Indian chief's cabin. Progress has no time to lose. The sun is shining. The air is ice-cold. Mouths blow columns of mist. Someone shouts. Sitting Bull emerges from his cabin. His face looks drained; the past reaches us devoid of colour. When they tell him they've come to arrest him, he replies that he needs time to get dressed, and that he'll come with them.

The dogs howl. The light crackles. A few Indian warriors remonstrate with the police officers. Very soon, there's mayhem. People hurl abuse at the police, there's a scuffle; and at that point no one knows what happened. Dramas sweep up their witnesses with them. A man produces a gun and fires. A mouth quivers. Reality has vanished, everything is happening at once, exploding. Fighting breaks out. An arm waves furiously. A man falls to the ground, his eye swivels in the straw and the cold dust; suddenly, a police officer shoots point-blank. Sitting Bull teeters. Perhaps he can hear the catcalls rising for the last time from the bleachers; he's a dead thing, but he can still see the horrible small faces of men who are alive. And then, another police officer steps forward and finishes him off with a rifle shot. Someone rolls the body over with a foot.

———————

AFTER THAT, the Indians packed up their felt and leather tents, the tatters, old blankets and bags, the little that remained to them. The children cried. The wind blew into the wagons. A hoarse voice yelled an instruction to start moving. Bile rose briefly in their throats. Fleeing their village, the Lakota found refuge in Big Foot's encampment; but General Miles immediately ordered his arrest. The Army delayed. There was a flurry of commands and countermands. Big Foot was a pacifist, and it would probably be better to trust him and allow things to calm down.

But fearing the arrival of the soldiers, the Lakota, along with Big Foot's Miniconjou, were on the move again. It was horribly cold, they made slow progress beneath the frozen trees, and along the mountain ridges. Big Foot was ill. Many of the children were ill. They waded across the mouth of Cherry Creek, and then followed an old wagon trail along the Cheyenne River. The horses walked slowly beneath the cold rain. The riders advanced in silence, followed by a long procession of old nags, men and women on foot, and carts. People pant and grumble. The track is so crowded that the horses miss their footing; the procession moves off again. Everyone is alone, alone with their own weariness. They halt in the late afternoon, any old where, in a jumble of tents and clustered cabins.

It was at that point that General Miles deployed two cavalry regiments to cut off the convoy of fugitives. In the meantime the Indians had set off again, dragging themselves along, and starving. The wind swept across the plain. Faces hardened, skin turned grey. Women and children huddled in the corner of a wagon beside a few stalks of rotting straw. A few hours later, below Porcupine Butte, they came across a group of cavalrymen; the two hundred men from the 7th cavalry regiment led by Major Whitside, the Little Big Horn regiment, the one that was wiped out when they were defeated by Sitting Bull. Oh! they weren't the same men of course, but it was the same outfit, steeped in the same tradition. The regiment cut off the escape route for a convoy of dying Indians. One of the Indians waved a white flag, a piece of cloth on the end of a pike. Someone asked the soldiers for milk and something to eat; the soldiers promised to distribute basic supplies at Wounded Knee River.

They set off again, escorted by the cavalry. Once they arrived, an officer ordered the Indians to make camp for the night. Big Foot, who was worse, was taken to the infirmary. He wore only a shirt and a scarf, and he was cold. Very cold. The Indians put up shelters for themselves as best they could, and the soldiers distributed flour and bacon. Families clustered around small braziers. They cut slices of bacon, which they held over the flames. The bacon sizzled and the fat ran. The smoke stank. The children stared at the fire; their faces glowed as the pine logs blazed. A little water rolled around and lapped in the bottom of the cooking pots. Then, night fell. The wagons creaked in the wind. The men remained standing for a while, until they were cut down by exhaustion. And once again it was cold, even colder.

———————

IN THE MORNING OF 29TH DECEMBER, a bugle sounded. The warriors were summoned and ordered to hand over their firearms. But fearing that there were still some hidden weapons, the soldiers searched the tents. They barged their way into the wagons looking for knives, hatchets, anything they could lay their hands on. Anger mounted. A squadron kept their guns trained on the Indians from the top of the hill. Suddenly, a shot was fired. There was a skirmish; no one knows where it started; and then there was a terrible rumbling which immediately drowned out all other noise. It was four Hotchkiss mountain guns. Easily reloaded, manoeuvrable, exceptionally accurate at a range of two kilometres, they were positioned on the hilltop above the encampment.

Then everything changed. A few Indians who had managed to get behind the line of rifles launched themselves at the soldiers. There was violent hand-to-hand fighting. Bayonets slashed arms, bounced off skulls. Orders were bawled that no one could hear. The mountain guns fired at random on the tents. The wooden frames collapsed in cinders. People were running everywhere. Wagons gave way under the weight of the bodies in them. Then the guns started firing towards the plain to catch the runaways.

Suddenly, the noise had stopped. The silence was like a banner flapping in the wind. The soldiers lowered their rifles. What was happening? There was something alarming about the silence. The soldiers looked at each other, struck dumb.

Below them, the Indians were almost all dead. When the guns were reloaded, there were two or three more explosions. Then shouts; a few soldiers begged for it to stop. There was even a howl, but who it came from, nobody knows.

And that was all.

A violent storm blew up. Snow fell from the sky like a divine ordinance. The snowflakes whirled around the dead Indians, light and untroubled. They landed on hair and lips. Every eyelid was spangled with hoar frost. What a delicate thing a snowflake is! It's like a weary little secret, a forlorn and inconsolable touch of gentleness.

Then came the wind, with a terrifying hum, pitch dark and flitting mountain tops. It snatched the soldiers' breath away as they advanced. The snow was so heavy that a little farther on they had to retreat into their quarters and wait it out. They tried to sleep. Two days passed. When the storm had calmed a little, they emerged again and were met with a horrible surprise. All around, there were corpses. And nothing else. The plain was covered with dead Indians.

The soldiers requisitioned a number of civilians. Huge farmers' carts rolled into the wrecked encampment. It was a grim harvest. You don't often see that kind of cart filled with dead bodies. Stiffened hands protruded from between the bars. The flesh had frozen.

A burial pit was required. The pickaxe struck the earth, winter's thin layer of permafrost. Eventually, the soil became softer, warmer. Once the spades had stopped their scraping, three men jumped down into the hole. It all took time; the dead were passed, one by one, from one man to the next, and stripped of everything that could be sold. They were seized by the arms and legs: One, two, three! Whee! and thrown into empty space. The men were dizzy from exhaustion and from the stench that rose around them. The bodies piled up, the men worked on, scarves over their mouths. They whistled and passed round a plug of tobacco during their break. And then it was back to work, the arms, the feet and the body lobbed into the pit. A sleeping man. Another sleeping man, and another; they're all asleep! Their heads lolling to one side and their arms stuck awkwardly under their bellies. And each with that face, that dead stare, like a horse's eye. A hundred. That's a hundred corpses. A hundred and one, a hundred and two, a hundred and three. They stacked eighty-four men, forty-four women and eighteen children. First one row which was covered with old blankets, and then another laid in the other direction; and so on. It was 2nd January 1891.

Buying a Child

IT'S SAID THAT ARCHILOCHUS walked across a desert of bones and that he was obliged to make the journey alone. An Indian physician, Dr Charles Eastman, had come to scour the area for survivors. He'd arrived one morning, 1st January, and by midday he and the men who were with him had found ten people. They continued to search through the undergrowth, anxious, but full of love and sorrow, going everywhere a dying person might have hidden; when, all of a sudden, they thought they heard a baby's cry. They assumed they must have dreamt it, but there was a second whimper. So the men spread into a line, moving forward slowly, stopping to cock an ear. The sky was grey, the clouds were thick. The men walked in silence. Suddenly one of them called out. The others hurried over. The crying came from a woman's corpse. They dropped onto all fours, and scraped around the dead woman. They lifted up her body, stiff, cold and congealed in its own blood; in her dead arms, they found a little girl. They had to use force to prise apart the frozen arms.

———————

WHILE THE REGIMENT was slaughtering the Indians at Wounded Knee, Buffalo Bill had landed in America, and then reached Nebraska. There he had learned of the death of Sitting Bull and the massacre which had just taken place. It's claimed that to the end of his days he regretted that he hadn't been able to intervene. That's as may be. The key fact is that he immediately made his way to Wounded Knee. You can see him in a legendary photograph, at Pine Ridge, with General Miles. It can't be said that this connection bodes well. Miles was a scumbag. He'd had the Apache scouts in his own army deported to Florida; and Geronimo, who had given himself up only on condition that he would be able return to his own territory after two years of captivity, never saw Arizona again. A few years later,

Miles would put down the strikes in the Pullman factories in Chicago; twelve factory workers would be killed. Miles would die in 1925, from a heart attack, in Washington DC. Attending a circus performance with his grandchildren.

It was a few days after Buffalo Bill's arrival that the young Leonard W. Colby, an admired soldier and a womanizer, found himself at Pine Ridge railway station. Later, when he had attained a fair degree of celebrity, Leonard W. Colby used repeatedly to tell the story of how Buffalo Bill had escorted him to Pine Ridge, accompanied by John Burke, his impresario, and how, as they rode along together and talked, they had eventually caught up with the reserves. After leaving their bags in the white army tents, between the stocks of gunpowder and the barrels of bacon, Leonard Colby and Buffalo Bill went on to Wounded Knee. But as soon as they climbed the hill and saw the plain littered with burnt-out wagons and a swarm of vermin, booty-hunters and scavengers, all in search of Indian goods, Leonard Colby and Buffalo Bull, both of whom had experience of war and had seen battlefields before, instantly realized that what had taken place was not a battle, but a full-scale massacre.

Afterwards they went to the Pine Ridge trading post and then to the bar where Buffalo Bill was a regular because May Asay, the queen of Pine Ridge, was his mistress. I don't know if May Asay actually enjoyed being kissed by Buffalo Bill in the outhouse next to her shop, or if she liked feeling his big military moustache against her lips. I don't know if she liked being fucked on the dusty table, wiping herself with a dusty dishrag, and then returning behind the counter to allow her climax to subside. What I do know is that James Asay, her husband, had distributed whisky to the soldiers the night before the massacre. He ran a business, and it needed to make money; a little present to the troops couldn't do any harm.

However, James Asay was perhaps not entirely immune to scruples. He would start boozing in the morning, and by midday his life had liquefied into oblivion. He slept all afternoon, sweating between filthy sheets and calling to some shadowy figure in his sleep. His wife would drag him roughly out of his bed in the evening, and pack him off to mind the bar. You can see that there are many ways a man can be snared in the coils of his own existence; and Asay, who had gone and given barrels of whisky to the cavalry regiment at Wounded Knee in order to win their custom, is now crushed under the weight of his own self, right there, in the middle of the afternoon, and, with his flesh pinned fast to his own nullity, it's impossible to hate him entirely. You can imagine his forehead sticky with sweat, his cadaverous breath, his pallor, you can imagine how horribly alone he is when he's with other people, and even when he's not, perpetually alone and in anguish. Maybe he's a man to be pitied. Yes, he certainly pitied himself! He wanted to act the way they do in books, to throw himself into the abyss of his own being and end it all. But he hadn't read any books, and he hated them. All his intelligence had turned against him in the form of alcohol, tobacco, indolence and unfortunate business deals.

General Miles came into the bar from time to time, and the queen of Pine Ridge was uneasy on these occasions. Miles would drink, become progressively mean and physically violent. He'd get completely sozzled, knock the tables over and, twisting her arm, try to drag her off to the outhouse. She was a little afraid of the old piss artist. And even though Buffalo Bill spent his nights boozing and playing cards, she preferred his ridiculous baritone voice, his goatee beard and his tasselled jackets, because he was gentler. But General Miles wasn't at Pine Ridge that day; there was only Leonard Colby, Buffalo Bill and Major John Burke, the impresario.

When Leonard Colby talked afterwards about the Pine Ridge episode, he never—but never—talked about the night he spent in Asay's bar in the company of Buffalo Bill and Burke. He was nonetheless capable of saying all sorts of things to impress his audience, or to con journalists and the Indians he sometimes did business with, but he never told how Burke, with his ugly great mug, had talked to him, for the first time, between two rounds of hooch, about the little Indian girl. No, that he never talked about. He never said a word about the discussion where Burke first mentioned Zintkala Nuni, a tiny baby found at Wounded Knee, a little girl, "the most interesting Indian relic of all", a tiny infant discovered a few days after the drama, who had survived by a miracle (and you can imagine with horror how Burke managed to emphasize the word, like a puppet nodding its head). No, Leonard Colby never talked about it, not to the journalists, nor to the guests in his grand sitting room, nor to anyone else. He never said how much Burke had paid—a pretty stiff price, it's said, but Burke didn't want people to know this either, and he kept it secret throughout his life—because Burke had bought the child. Yes, he had doubtless bought it for the Wild West Show. Well, perhaps not. But why else would he have done it, if it wasn't to put the baby on show and add a sensational number to his programme: The Tiny Survivor of Wounded Knee? And then Buffalo Bill and John Burke must have changed their minds and decided to resell the child. We'll never know why.

At that moment, General Colby's heart started to beat very fast. He'd smelled a bargain. What could be better for his trafficking with the Indians than to adopt a little squaw? And since there's no incompatibility between business and tears—on the contrary—because hoodlums, being the world's orphans, are violent and sentimental, he doubtless felt a mix of self-interest and sentiment. The bargaining was fierce. Sitting in Asay's store, right next to the baby who was held close by an Indian woman, while May, the queen of Pine Ridge, poured drinks, Colby, Buffalo Bill and Colby negotiated a price for the child. No one knows how much Colby paid for Zintkala Nuni, but it doesn't matter; we know only that he was mad, and that more than once in his life his behaviour bordered on insanity; but his greatest act of lunacy was undoubtedly to buy the child and adopt it, and in so doing to mix tears and profit to an extreme degree. Yes—as you can see on that dreadful photograph where he's holding the child in his arms, dressed in a sort of christening robe—you could say that Leonard Colby advanced a long way into his insanity, swallowing up the life of another person in his own life, and dissolving his in a calamitous enterprise.

———————

THEY CALLED THE LITTLE Indian girl Marguerite, Marguerite Colby. I've seen pictures of the child, she must be four or five years old. In one of them she's wrapped in a lace or muslin curtain, standing by a sofa. Her face is dark. Her eyes are black. She's very pretty. She's wearing a dress fit for a princess, as they do in good families. She's smiling timidly, her hand has grasped a bit of the curtain and she's holding it between her fingers, like an enigma. The Colbys' house was full of dubious antiques, ostrich feathers, lotus flowers and hieroglyphs. Afternoon tea was served with sandwiches, fruit tarts and jam cookies. Everyone was eager to know the details of the little Indian girl's life, and Mrs Colby, her adoptive mother, started a column in the newspaper about the doings of her daughter. You can see that, from the very start, the mass media had a propensity for excess.

And the little girl grew bigger and unruly, and she never became the model of good Christian upbringing that people wished. When she was still very young, and still playing tag among the washing lines in the yard behind the house, she would hang around in the alleyway with the negro women chattering under the porch. Then, from the boarding school where she was eventually sent, she wrote long, incoherent letters to her mother; she was often ill, and sometimes threatened to kill herself. In the end, her mother took her to Portland where they set up home. As for her adoptive father, Leonard Colby, they never saw him. He was far away, wheeling and dealing his way through life. For a while he used the name of Zintkala Nuni as a calling card in his truck with the Indians; it was a profitable tactic.

When you make a stained-glass window, you begin by outlining shapes and agonies of colour. And then you cut out the pieces of glass and you apply the blues, the reds, the yellows, and you bake it all. Once it's cooled, you stick a little bit of blue glass—a blueberry blue— to a bit of red; and that creates the outline of a hill, Hollywood, cinema's colonial outpost. This was where the young Indian woman settled later on, in return for a few dollars. In those days, cameramen loaded their cameras as fast as they could, films were churned out like hot dogs, actors were yelled at to take up their damn positions, and when the emulsion was exposed to the light while the cameraman furiously cranked the handle, a latent image of cowboys and Indians with horses and stagecoaches took shape—a bit like the way in spring, before their flowers burst open, buds give magnolias a hint of colour. But audiences had

had enough of Westerns filmed in New Jersey with phoney cowboys and fake Indians, and they wanted the little square of celluloid to be coated for real with dust, and its eighteen by twenty-four millimetres to be tattooed for real by sun from the West.

The young woman performed in a few films. But if genuine Indians were required, it wasn't for the leading roles. So, within a few months of arriving, she found herself destitute. It was then that, by some strange fate, she was recruited for the opening parade of the Wild West Show. Equipped with a feather boa and flashy jewellery, she probably had to dance and show her legs. She knew none of the details of her own history.

Eventually, after chasing bit parts for a few years, and finding that life, apparently, had nothing to offer her, she abandoned herself to various sordid misadventures, and, in order to pay the rent on her room and buy herself the sandwiches she lived on, she resorted to prostitution. And then, the Spanish flu, which was rife at the time and picked on weaker creatures, carried her off.

There's a photograph of her taken shortly before she died. She's posing as an Indian in the San

Francisco Panama–Pacific International Exhibition. And it's strange, but in this photograph, although she's Indian, she looks as though she's wearing a *disguise*. And if Zintkala Nuni looks travestied in this wretched commercial image, it's not only because the sad, worn look in her eye screams through her costume and the circus setting that we will all die burned by our masks. No, it's not only because she's been kitted out in a tasselled shirt and cheap moccasins. It's something far more terrible. If, dressed like this, Zintkala Nuni, the child of Wounded Knee, looks as though she's wearing a disguise—it's because she's no longer Indian.

The "Battle" of Wounded Knee

THERE WAS YET ANOTHER WAY in which Buffalo Bill had turned his stay in Nebraska to advantage. Before resuming his famous show, he'd been on a pilgrimage to the place where Sitting Bull was murdered. He'd met the family of the old Indian chief and he'd told them how much affection and respect he had for him. It was quite sincere. Perhaps he felt the grandeur of something that he had sensed before, when he was a humble scout, in the reality of his own life. But this must have seemed very distant now. It must have appeared strange, after seeing so many people cluster on the bleachers like grains of corn shaken out by an invisible hand! So, in exchange for a few dollars, and perhaps also out of affection, the Indians had handed over the cabin where Sitting Bull lived, and he'd had it dismantled and transported by train to his ship. And then he'd also haggled for the last horse belonging to the Indian chief. Finally, passing by Wounded Knee again, he'd gathered up the last remnants of the Lakota tribe who were lingering nervously in the vicinity of the massacre, and he'd signed them up. No doubt it was a way of saving their lives.

The return voyage must have been long. First there was thick fog, followed by heavy, deep blue clouds, whose dark blue grew ever deeper. Then lightning tore the horizon, and this lasted a day and a night. In the morning, while he was alone on deck, he noticed a sandy island in the distance. The wind whipped his face. Behind a strand of mist, the sun began to dazzle him. He shaded his eyes awkwardly with his hand, staring ahead at the great empty expanse and the tall, wild waves. Gusts of wind slashed his throat, and he continued to stare. The wind tipped the ship to one side, and the waves smashed against its steel flanks. Their crests shone white. Suddenly, Buffalo Bill thought he saw something, a tiny shiver on the surface of the world. It was whales. For several hours they followed the boat at a distance, apparently indifferent, then disappeared from sight. The weather was fine, the ship glided imperturbably over the water; they were the masters of life. Buffalo Bill stood in the prow and the air filled his cheeks as if he were about to blow into a flute, like the boy in Manet's painting, with his circus jacket and his puffy trousers.

Several times a day, he would go down into the hull and see to the old Indian chief's horse himself. He rubbed its back with a wisp of straw and sluiced out its stall. Then he'd go back up on deck and look at the sea. He sensed a strange violence beneath its gentle surface, beneath the sparkling shapes which the ship broke open before crashing into the foam. He loved the silver waves, but also the long silences, the dead sun. The seagulls perched on the masts, little spots of white. One night, the storm was so harsh, the sea so wild, that he began to feel afraid. At times, he felt he was dissolving into the sky.

AS SOON AS HE ARRIVED back in Europe, the performances of the Wild West Show started up again. He added two new acts. In the first, you can see a group of Indians in the middle of the arena.

The spectators have hired opera glasses for a few coins, and they look. No one knows yet what's going to happen. The crowd is impatient and jostles with curiosity. Behind the warriors you can make out a sort of cabin and there's an older Indian standing in the doorway. He's a chieftain, which you can tell from his crown of feathers.

Suddenly, Buffalo Bill enters the arena. He does one circuit on horseback and bows. The applause rings out. Women stand up on their seats amid the smell of creosote and horse droppings. The presenter then announces an extraordinary episode: "The death of Sitting Bull with his real horse and his real cabin, retrieved by Buffalo Bill himself." So that's what it was! Nothing can stop the demon of performance. Nothing can fill the cash registers fast enough. And immediately the curious crowd presses forward, people want a better view. You can never see enough. There's something grand and fine, or perhaps very horrible and very vulgar, that will always escape us. You think you're going to see it right here, right now! And you absolutely mustn't miss it, otherwise you'll never see it again. You stand there, like the knight of the Round Table before whose eyes the lance of salvation and the Holy Grail are about to pass. And like him, dazed and bemused, you watch them go by, and you forget to reach out your hand and take them.

All of a sudden the horsemen emerge from the wings. They do one circuit in a frantic stampede. But they're no longer Indian police officers, they're a detachment from the US Army; fiction has these approximations which falsify everything. Galloping past a long strip of painted canvas, the cavalry-men fire their revolvers. The air is thick with dust. The Indians open fire in return; the cavalry slowly retreats to the far end of the arena. But after a few moments, the cavalrymen charge again, and, once they're close to the cabin, some of them dismount and hide behind the artfully arranged bales of straw. An Indian falls down dead, then another, and another one still. The soldiers advance under a hail of bullets. It's at this point that Sitting Bull—it's not him, but an actor—heroically mounts his steed. He does two circuits, performing all kinds of pointless acrobatics in the stifling heat. Suddenly, hurling himself at the soldiers, Sitting Bull shoots point-blank and wounds a man in the face. The fellow collapses.

Another fires back. Then the Indian chief is hit and falls off his horse. He crawls behind a clump of trees, dried reeds woven through a wattle fence. The Indian hides, but everyone can see him. The soldiers slowly move closer, they don't know where the Indian is! The crowd shouts. And whistles. Chins quiver. A bag of chips slips down between the bleachers. The curtain of destiny has been drawn back, and any minute now it might close again! A young soldier crawls over to the right, Sitting Bull hasn't seen him... Every breath is held. The Indian looks round, he barely has time to move before the soldier fires. Silence. A second shot hits him full in the stomach and the Indian staggers. Ah! how people all love him now, or at least the children do, and even the adults secretly feel that precipitate of irremediable guilt which ultimately absolves one of everything. The Indian is dead. The cavalrymen climb back into the saddle and leave the arena. The crowd applauds and calls for an encore; because right now, what people want more than anything else is to see the scene again. Yes, just the tragic end, just that part, the death of the Indian chief. Emotion is geared to arrive on command; the same episode watched repeatedly, or the looped refrain from a song, bring tears to our eyes every time, as if a sublime and inexpressible truth were being repeated unchanged. So the actor stands up again, the dead revive, the cavalrymen return; and they all perform the finale for a second time. After doing a circuit of the arena, the Indian once again falls off his horse, once again he hides behind the clump of trees, once again the crowd shouts out, but perhaps a little louder, with even more feeling than the first time. A child cries. It's so much better than it was a few moments earlier, so much more powerful, so much truer. Knowing the end doesn't change a thing. In fact it adds to the turmoil, as if surprise and frenzy are intensified when they're rehashed. But as soon as the Indian chief is dead for a second time, as soon as he's landed once more face first in the dust, and the crowd has felt the tremendous frisson that comes from seeing him die *again*, everyone gets up from their seats, their hearts aglow; and they rush to the refreshment stall to buy sweets or something to drink.

DURING THE INTERVAL, people wait impatiently for the next episode while they talk to each other about the first one. Everybody wants to tell everybody else about what they saw, the tiny crumb of truth they think is theirs. And in almost identical words, they bang on unstoppably to each other about the same scraps of the adventure. And then the bell rings. They're being called back to their seats. The spectacle is about to start again. Buffalo Bill is still in his tent, taking a moment's rest. Lord, a spectacle goes on for a long time! But once you're on the stage, you don't feel the time passing. The gaze from the crowd freezes the clock hands. Everything stops. You're in eternity. Buffalo Bill loves it; he loved it from the minute he took his first uncertain steps on Broadway after fetching up there by chance. He'd had such stage fright! He'd spoken his lines in a faltering voice, walking stiffly across the stage and making exaggerated gestures. But he's moved on since then. At present, he knows exactly what to do. He enters the arena on horseback and everyone looks at him. Everyone! That does something to you. He's no longer an actor like any other, he's the most famous character on the planet. Ah! it must be strange to be adored like that.

Not many people had had that experience before. He barely has to do a thing. All eyes are on him, Buffalo Bill. But he's not just the incarnation of his character, the outermost shadow of his soul. No. He has drawn flame from the earth, deluged the world with leaflets, publicity and magazines, where, line by line, his legend has been constructed and polished, the *apologia pro vita sua* made ever more ingenious. And all this for an exemplary product, an exemplarily American product, a magnificent contribution to the History of Civilization.

Right now, families are threading their way past the refreshment stalls and returning to their seats. The young men look at the girls parading in their lacy blouses and they help them climb onto their bench. Everyone is here, on the bleachers, in the sunshine. The gates of pleasure stand before them. And what is Pleasure? Nobody knows. And nobody cares. We love the giddiness, we love being frightened, identifying with the characters, screaming, shouting, laughing and crying. Perhaps it's without any substance, but in the end this doesn't matter if it thrills and intoxicates us, if it allows our feelings to brush up against the heart

ÉRIC VUILLARD

of a hidden world. Spectacle draws its power and its dignity from being nothing. It leaves us irremediably alone, with no wound to see the light of day, no trace of evidence. And yet, in the midst of this noisy vacuum, in the great pity we feel, and even in our very scorn—there's something there. As if this grand ephemeral entertainment, this desperate forgetting of ourselves, this way of turning our heads to get a *better look* were one of the most tragic moments of our being: devoid of any sign or revelation; and where all that happens is that the heart feels a pang, a hand clutches hold of another person, any old person, as long as they're right next to us on the bleachers, and we can experience our adjacent anguish in a shout, a laugh, a simple community of feeling.

And now Frank Richmond announces something extraordinary, the greatest chapter in the story of the Wild West, a world monument! Shush! "Ladies and gentlemen, here, for the very first time, with the participants themselves, is the famous Battle of Wounded Knee!" People now understand the reason for Buffalo Bill's voyage, his hasty departure from Nancy, his visit to the scene of the drama, the survivors he recruited. It makes for a great line-up.

So the grand epic begins, and the dream starts up again. Hundreds of horsemen gallop past, raising clouds of dust. The floor of the arena has been thoroughly doused, but it makes no difference, and the sun beats down. Wonderment grows, the horsemen are too many to count, and people ask themselves how many the arena can hold. It's a hundred metres long and fifty metres wide! The spectators clap and shout. The crowd watches this simulacrum of a US Army regiment go by, their eyes popping out of their heads. Children push forward to get a better view. Hearts are beating. The truth is finally about to be revealed.

Yet, if you look closely, it's not much more realistic than a film by Georges Méliès. It's the same fakery, the same Conquests of the Pole, the same Knights of the Snows, the same Dancing Skeletons, the same Chloroform Fiends! But it doesn't matter because art is business here. Simple things have the biggest effect, and it's the irrelevant things that are the most important.

Right now the Indians are performing their final role. They're there, disguised beneath the most improbable costumes, in a fog of flies. And, as usual,

when they come on stage, an indistinct rumbling
starts up, a mix of curiosity and hostility. You can't do
without Indians if you want the show. But the audience is here to hate them; the reason people have
come is to see them and to hate them. Despite Buffalo
Bill's introductory patter, and though he praises
their bravery, and provides some derisory, if well-
meaning commentary about their customs, the audience doesn't give a damn. It's not long since General
Sherman—who today sits astride four or five tons
of bronze on the most prestigious drive in Central
Park—declared that the Sioux should all be extermi-
nated: men, women and children. Hadn't he vowed
to remain in the West until all the Indians, absolutely
all of them—and these are his own words—had been
killed or deported? And wasn't it also he who decided
to wipe out the herds of bison, which were the prin-
cipal resource of the Indian tribes, in order to ensure
the speedy progress of the railroad? And wasn't it as
a hunter of bison that Buffalo Bill himself, hired by a
railroad company, first became known and acquired
his name?

You have only to look at a photograph of Cornelius
Vanderbilt, the emperor of the railroad, to understand

all this. You have only to study his mouth, the intractable purse of his lips, the cynical presumption. You have only to stare into his eyes to glimpse the desiccated little shrub inside. And you only have to contemplate the terrible portrait of General Sherman bequeathed to us by Mathew Brady—the one where he's in uniform, his arms folded, the eyes hard and his face ravaged by a kind of leprosy—to see the other side of the fable. Hatred.

We're the audience. It's us watching the Wild West Show. In fact we've always been watching it. We should be suspicious of our intelligence, suspicious of our refinement, and we should be suspicious too of our unscathed lives and the grand spectacle of our emotions. The maestro is there, inside us, standing right next to us. Visible and invisible. With his ideas that are as true they are false, his accommodating rhetoric.

And the spectacle starts again. The cavalrymen spin ferociously round in the arena. The dust turns your eyes red. A soldier tumbles to the ground, dead, then gets up and dusts off his jacket—the show continues. The cavalry surrounds the Indians.

The bleachers are packed out with twenty thousand people, more perhaps. Suddenly, a cavalryman leans over, and performs a few acrobatics on his circus horse. Bang! The Indians open fire; the noise is deafening and the air is too thick to breathe. They launch into fierce hand-to-hand combat, knives slash throats, men fall under the horses' hooves. A ranger advances under a hail of bullets. The audience looks on, mesmerized.

A few Indians ride around the rangers, yelling the way Buffalo Bill taught them to. They slap the palms of their hands over their mouths, Woo! Woo! Woo! And it makes a sort of wild, inhuman whoop. But this war cry was never heard on the Great Plains, nor in Canada, nor anywhere else—it's sheer invention on the part of Buffalo Bill. And what they don't yet know is that they will have to produce this war cry, this wonderful circus-act invention, on every stage and on every film set where they are hired as extras in depictions of their own misfortune. Yes, they're still unaware of the destiny that awaits the circus trick devised by Buffalo Bill, they cannot conceive that all children in the Western world will forever afterwards dance round the fire, flapping their palms over their mouths to produce "Indian war cries"; they can't imagine the prodigious future that awaits this monstrous thing, the fabulous power to combust the senses by means of spectacle. And yet, they must secretly have felt the full horror of it.

John Burke is bawling on the sidelines, his moustache drooping with spittle. He vociferates, and strides up and down, the way that nowadays overweight coaches wave their arms and yell at athletes to outdo themselves, demanding feats that they, as coaches, would be quite incapable of pulling off. His smart suit is caked in dust. His hair is plastered with sweat. The sleeves of his jacket are all sticky. He barks at the Indians to retreat. He angrily jabs his finger towards the far end of the arena. So, obeying instructions, the Indians withdraw, and some of them even launch into a desperate flight. But a few continue to resist. The soldiers valiantly withstand their attacks. The sun screams down. Everything goes dark. Eyes mist over, fists grip the bars of a chair. John Burke drops his cigarette. Hey! Ginger, watch out! An Indian jumps off his horse and fires at the soldier. He's a young fellow with red hair, an innocent, and he collapses in a stunt where his entire body seems to disappear. There's shouting. The earth turns red. There's been a catastrophe, the soldiers move off and huddle in a corner of the arena. The smell of gunpowder is suffocating. Vision blurs. But suddenly, Buffalo Bill erupts from backstage. Although his hair is now white, he displays a savage energy. He doesn't look the least constrained by the suit he's wearing, and in fact he stands out from his surroundings in a kind of vibration. His body doesn't belong in the arena, he's away on the Great Plains, elusive and resplendent.

In a whirlwind of dust he storms across the hundred metres separating him from the group of Indians who are about to get the better of the cavalry, and in a tremendous turnaround, he shoots fifteen savages in just a few seconds. The floor of the arena is covered in dead bodies. Encouraged by their hero, the cavalry rallies and suddenly the combat reverses the previous outcome. The military restore battle formation. They charge and the Indians withdraw, but there's only a handful of them left and they die one by one in a well-practised choreography. Things are now as far away from the original event as they could be, and the massacre has been transformed into a succession of thrilling exploits that lead to an edifying conclusion.

When the "battle" of Wounded Knee has finally ended, most of the Indians are dead. It's a crushing victory. Buffalo Bill bends over a wounded man, and then another. The scene is almost touching. Finally, he pays homage to the Indian combatants and raises them from the dead with an imperious gesture, before announcing the next act.

————————

THE SPECTACLE IS OVER; people wander round the Indian craft stalls and the hot-dog stands. They glance at the goods and try on a necklace. They'd love to have a tomahawk or even a feather headdress! This is what we now call merchandising. The Indians are selling products that derive from their genocide. They haggle with the gawpers, and then stash the modest sums in their leather purses.

Reality shows are not, as has been claimed, the ultimate, cruel and all-consuming incarnation of mass entertainment. They are its origin; they propel every last one of the participants of their dramas into perpetual amnesia. The survivors of Wounded Knee will have to endure for all eternity the blanks fired by General Miles's rangers, by night as well as by day, because, thanks to its giant projectors, the Wild West Show was the first artificially lit spectacle in the world, the first night-time spectacle.

From then on, whether in Strasbourg or in Illinois, in show after show, the survivors of Wounded Knee would perform the "soft" version of Wounded Knee. A version where the Indians and the 7th cavalry regiment would heroically confront each other, and where the US Army would emerge victorious. And for more than a year, right across Europe, they would perform the Buffalo Bill interpretation of the facts. In this edited version you don't see the stockbreeders' treachery, nor the ambush laid by Riley Miller who killed as many Indians as he could before flogging off their tunics and their scalps to Charles Bristol, to be included in the little display of relics at the Universal Exposition in Chicago. It's a version of the massacre, revised and corrected in true American spirit by Buffalo Bill and John Burke. It's the version for our school history books. A children's version. These theatricals don't include the Sioux's long and exhausting trek as they fled their reserve, nor the manoeuvres by the rangers to draw them meekly, in their dying hordes, to Wounded Knee. Nor does it include the Hotchkiss gun and its miracle of technology. Nor the snowstorm, nor the communal grave, nor the women, nor the children.

The Town of Cody

THE END OF THE WORLD IS APPROACHING.
And this time it's for real, it's not the wild imag-
inings of prophets or cloistered nuns, it's a wide-
spread impression, a commercial necessity—a wish.
Something is happening, something that's never
been seen before. It's as though every poor wretch in
the world had suddenly decided to head for America.
In 1870, there were forty million Americans; but by
1880 the number had gone up to fifty million; and by
1900 it was seventy-six million. That's a lot of inhabitants arriving and getting born in such a short space
of time, a population that's doubled in size in thirty
years, a territory that's expanding, a vast populace
turning up and filling out the place and propelling its
mistakes way out before it. In Minnesota, Missouri,
Arkansas, they're all gripped by a kind of madness.
No more quiet Sunday afternoons. Giddy up! we're
off to Oklahoma! Kansas! But in Kansas the safety

curtain is already burning, people are saying that gold has been found in California, and now everyone is making a dash for the Pacific: wagons, tramps, tarts, good-for-nothings of all kinds, but also prodigal sons, decent lads from Memphis who all want to *see*. And when they get there, what do they see? The perpetuity of the breakers, Big Sur, tremendous cliffs.

Nothing is easy for these people, but everything is possible. The human species has just embarked on a journey without end. People walk for months, they gallop, and then the rail tracks extend in an unprecedented war between Vanderbilt, Gould and two or three other crooks. There had to be a way of crossing the continent. And while the US Army labours at the expansion of Progress, the great powers rise up. Frenzied speculation. Scandalous bankruptcy. Legendary collusion. And all the while, people go from Duluth to Tacoma, from Houston to Los Angeles and from Chicago to San Francisco. The Union Pacific smashes through the Rockies and steams onward! From now on you can go everywhere without getting your feet wet. Oh! there'll be a few attacks and disruptions, but you can still travel all the way from the statue of Commodore Cornelius Vanderbilt in

New York City to San Francisco, while you read your newspaper.

In 1895, like any self-respecting American, Buffalo Bill created a town, investing his burgeoning fortune in a project for the future. And, bizarrely, he gave the town his real name: Cody. A town that came into being out of nowhere, as you can see on the photographs. At what point can you begin to speak of a town? In America in those days, towns flared up and died like wicks in a lamp. In 1900, the town of Cody was still just a few scattered hovels. Around 1903, Buffalo Bill Cody—it's hard to know what to call him now—built the Irma Hotel, named after his daughter. Its cherrywood bar was a gift from Queen Victoria. On the wall, rifles were a reminder of his past glories on the battlefield. John Burke had overseen all the details with devoted and sensitive attention. Business is a form of insanity. A yawning abyss. It's all anyone can see now. Life outside of it barely exists; nothing is safe from the gales that blow up out of the void. The entire world ends up in the stock exchange and the trading pit.

Cody is a stage set. It speaks the truth by lying. From a distance it looks hazy and insubstantial; it's bathed in an atmosphere of unease and unreality. This is because the town of Cody is dead. Completely and utterly dead. For nearly a hundred and seventy days a year the temperature in Cody remains below zero. And then it's got every possible kind of fake Western architectural feature: rustic balustrades, ugly brick house fronts, slot machines, rodeo girls. There's nothing in Cody. Just an all-consuming sadness.

At the time of Wounded Knee, four years had passed since Buffalo Bill had created Cody. He was very attached to the place, especially as it was his second project involving a town. You can't fail a thousand times. You have to create towns where people come to live—it's absolutely indispensable. Just as spectacles demand an audience, so a town needs inhabitants. But Cody didn't develop. Buffalo Bill was unable to apply to anything else the flair and the luck he demonstrated on the stage. But he would really have loved to turn his circus-performer's instincts into a town, a pretty little town, a town that was his and his alone; but which was also inhabited, luxurious even, full of life and movement and tourists and businesses; and bore his name. But it hadn't worked.

The town just stagnated in its stone-built decor. And then, it's said that in response to his request, Teddy Roosevelt, an old chum of Buffalo Bill, launched the construction of Shoshone Dam, the biggest dam of its time, and that suddenly the town of Cody took off. But this is only hearsay.

Buffalo Bill was constantly on the road, and the town of Cody was like an old dream, an old gypsy's dream, a desire to anchor his life somewhere, and to give it a real shape. Perhaps, like Alexander before him, the old beast imagined creating a town where he could end his headlong rush through the world in the company of a young mistress, one last love, purer and sweeter than the rest—and be finally reconciled. So he had several short-lived affairs. He had the stubborn sorrow of victors, the secret pain of people who have had everything and imagine that they still deserve something more. He didn't know what. A town? A girl perhaps?

A lady of Venice was the greatest mirage of his life. At the age of almost forty he fell for a starlet. The story is banal, which makes it all the more profound. Everything relating to Buffalo Bill becomes such a cardboard cut-out that it's ultimately quite disarming. They met in London during the first European tour of the Wild West Show, which was a veritable triumph. The gigantic counterfeit creation had won over the most demanding audiences. She was in the crowd of spectators and it's not known how she came to his notice. The girl had just turned seventeen, and her name was Katherine. No sooner had he met her than a few days later, with a well-crafted mix of sincerity and grandiloquence, the old fox told her that she was "the most beautiful girl in the world". In these circumstances imagination counts for nothing, and it's the most hackneyed phrases that work the best. But Buffalo Bill didn't have time to finish the job, he had to go back to America; they wrote to each other. Very soon, she confessed her passion for the theatre, and came to join him. He was beginning to feel his age, but with her, he thought he felt a renewed enthusiasm. So he acquired the rights for a dreadful play, *A Lady of Venice*, and he took it to the best producer in New York.

The premiere was a disaster. The most favourably inclined journalists wrote that she had a pretty face and some expression, but that she didn't have an ounce of talent. Audiences didn't take to it either. Buffalo Bill had to bail out the producer; he spent several thousand dollars in an attempt to rescue the play. But it continued to lose money. It was terrible for him to encounter such resistance. For a long time, success had taught him to regard audiences as amenable, submissive entities; and now, all of a sudden, they weren't responding to him, he couldn't transfer his winning streak, the only star he could create was himself, and his only success was his show. He didn't know how to apply to other circumstances the magic formula he thought he possessed; all he actually possessed was his *métier*; chance had been responsible for the rest.

However, he did what he could. He listened to no one. Not to the newspapers, nor to his friends, nor to John Burke, who advised him to be careful. Buffalo Bill loved Katherine. He loved her delicate skin, her voice, her arse, her youth. For almost two months, the play toured from one town to the next without success; the tour had to be called off. Buffalo Bill refused to give up and immediately programmed another play, investing substantial sums of money—eighty thousand dollars!—with no hope of any return. The result was a series of resounding flops. The journalists let rip, as if they were taking their revenge for Buffalo Bill's unbroken success, as if they wanted to use this indirect withdrawal of their goodwill to show that they had always been independent, and that their generosity towards him had been something other than servility. Finally, the critics savagely exposed the liaison. But the old entertainer wanted to go on fighting his bad luck. In his dressing room, he would fix Katherine's full-length portrait with a melancholy stare. Ah! so he was the only person who could see those exquisitely slender ankles, that tilted face and the way she held a pen between her fingers!

But he wasn't the only person. A millionaire's son from New York also noticed them. And he married her. There were endless articles in the gutter press reporting that the young couple were blissfully happy. For Buffalo Bill the fountain of youth now ran bitter. But an old lion never loses heart. And although Katherine wanted for nothing, she was perhaps still fascinated by his charisma or excited by his theatrics, and she eventually started seeing her old mentor again. They met in squalid hotel bedrooms, with no thought for decency. It was like a second honeymoon;

after the rows and the reconciliations, they wept and were reunited, and Buffalo Bill showered his little chickadee with caresses and small gifts. He worshipped her. She was a princess, a Sunday princess. And then he wearied of her again. In despair, no doubt, at the mediocrity of her fate, Katherine would start her morning with two or three cocktails, and then carry on drinking through the day with brandy, champagne, and all the things that help you to forget a mean and thankless existence. Her husband filed for divorce.

The scandalmongers claim—but should we believe them?—that Buffalo Bill had other mistresses apart from this brash creature; and these weren't just an occasional lapse or a passing fancy. There were dozens of them. Everywhere his bohemian existence had taken him, he had whiled away entire nights propping up the bar in the company of a few miserable tarts; and from time to time the old entertainer would even carry off one of his nocturnal conquests for a few days or weeks. And John Burke would try to assess the possible consequences, the negative publicity, and in the morning or during the dreary afternoons, he would scour the acrimonious newspaper articles written by reactionary journalists. And as he stroked his huge whiskers he would calculate and recalculate the profit loss, the size of the hole in the kitty. With his plump hands he would leaf through the order books and the engagement diary for the Wild West Show, and frown. But however much he castigated Buffalo Bill, however much he warned him, or even lost his temper, the old fox doubtless believed, like so many other celebrities, that in all matters he had been granted a sort of grace or impunity. He was led by his pheromones, which exuded a heady perfume in the direction of his excessively tender heart, and when this happened Buffalo Bill was unable to restrain himself. He was sentimental and obscene. And yet, one fine day, after years of this vagabond existence and an assiduous patronage of brothels, the old clown, who was now sixty-four, perhaps finally sated, and most certainly tired, wrote—at the instigation of his daughter—to Louisa, his wife, to ask whether she would be willing to forget the past.

There's no such thing as forgetting. Forgiveness always comes with reservations. However, Louisa and Buffalo Bill did meet up again. They took a few trips together. There was a reconciliation. At the end of her life, Louisa's face was sour and mean. She had kept out of the frame, and she had felt her face whipped from afar by the cold plumage of fame, like an evil wind. They had undoubtedly loved each other once, but it was all so distant now. She had known William Cody and then Buffalo Bill, and she had felt this pathetic doubling gradually mutate into something else. This time, she hoped that William Cody, or Buffalo Bill, or both of them—it didn't matter which— would soon return for good, finally sated, and possibly grateful. Of course, there was more to it than feelings; she held her little reticule clutched tight, she kept a watchful eye on the family heritage, on her daughter, and all this figured in the calculations of her heart and the account book of her existence. But there was, undeniably, something else. Something that was never quite done with, something bitter and tender. After all, they had been together for a long time, and they were about to celebrate their forty-fifth wedding anniversary. He seemed weary of his vagabond existence, and she still seemed attached to her husband. It would, undoubtedly, be wrong to see this belated rapprochement as a capitulation on the part of an old roué. Long lives are mysteries that defy understanding. They have their ruses and their little ways. There's nothing anyone can say about them. A shared life is probably always a long succession of joys and misunderstandings. It's impossible for the sun to shine for ten, or even twenty years; winter exists too! Ripe fruit falls, the grass withers, and then all that's left is a little humus. But it's perhaps not nothing for one life to pronounce its verdict on another.

THERE REMAINS the little town of Cody, in its icy desert. Like a strange memory set in the middle of nowhere, an enigma, and nobody knows what it might teach us.

The town hasn't prospered much since its creation. With its eight thousand inhabitants, it serves as a stopover at the foot of the mountains. Today, next door to the Irma Hotel, which still exists, a small museum exhibits a motley collection of souvenirs:

firearms, posters for the Wild West Show, Indian objects, flora from the region and countless photographs of our hero. It's a rendezvous for all who love the Wild West. Cody is said to be the second most important town in Wyoming, a state that's half the size of France. Tourists flock in droves to India and Rajasthan, others take off for Bergamo to admire the Duomo and weep over Donizetti's grave, but anyone who has never seen Idaho Falls or a rodeo in Cody is an imbecile. There's nothing to beat munching a T-bone steak beneath a bison's head, and then buying country and western CDs in the local Walmart! Ah, Cody! You're like Buffalo Bill, a completely dead town. Yes, you're just another kind of ghost!

Reality Isn't What It Used to Be

AND BUFFALO BILL CARRIED ON indefatigably with his tours. He grew older on stage. Nothing would make him give up. He was hooked, smitten, addicted. There was no curing him. Yet almost everywhere, new distractions were emerging, new spectacles, new forms of rapture. The Wild West Show was beginning to look tacky.

From now on, during his long tours round the US, in seedy little towns where people still booked his show, Buffalo Bill would lodge with friends when he wasn't sleeping in his own tent. With age, friendships become precious. You see each other less often, but you're always glad to meet up. And so from time to time Buffalo Bill would spend a few days with his friend Elmer Dundy, an old chum. And while they chatted together in the large sitting room, recalling this or that episode from their life in Nebraska, little Elmer (in the US the eldest son often takes the father's first name, like a further proof of genealogy) would worm his way between the pompom-fringed lampshades and the leather armchairs. He'd listen in open-mouthed wonder—the way children look at the plaster figures on merry-go-rounds. He'd listen for hours to Buffalo Bill talking about his exploits, the sixty-nine bison he killed in a single day against Bill Comstock's forty-eight, and thanks to which he inherited the name Bill, which he stuck after Buffalo to commemorate the day. Elmer listened to him telling the tales he'd already told a thousand and one times about the Indian wars, his wild youth, how he embarked on a life of adventure at the age of fourteen, how his feet hurt riding mules without shoes, how Ned Buntline wrote the story of his life, the one that Elmer had read in the three-cent volume his father had bought for him. Yes, for hours on end, Elmer would listen to the old cheapskate rehashing this prodigious bunkum. He would listen to stories about rangers and edifying tales of battle. But what Elmer really wanted to hear, the thing that made his heart race for hours as he sat on the floor of the sitting room, hanging on the lips of Buffalo Bill, wasn't the description of the Eiffel Tower, nor the stories about Sitting Bull. It wasn't life in the Wild West, nor the death of Yellow Hair, nor the story of Little Big Horn. No. The only thing that genuinely interested little Elmer, the only real reason he had for listening to the old fart's claptrap, was that after a thousand yarns about Sitting Bull and the Pony Express, he always ended up talking about the Wild West Show.

What interested Elmer was the show, and only the show. He didn't give a monkey's about the stampedes in the desert, the saloons in Nebraska and the true adventures of Kit Carson, and although he couldn't have cared less about Indian customs and Indian victories, he nevertheless wanted to know everything about Sitting Bull's acting career, which interested him a whole heap more that the warrior's actual military exploits. For him the Indian chief was part of folklore, and he didn't care what his role at Little Big Horn had been; it was of no interest that Sitting Bull was an approximate and idiotic translation of Tatanka Iyotanka, which means "male bison rolling in the dust"; his legendary silence was of no interest, nor was his accuracy with a bow and arrow; it was of no interest that he killed his first bison at the age of ten, that he fought in his first battle at the age of fourteen and shot a man off his horse; the white eagle's feather and the name given to him by his father were of no interest—none of these things, which are so vital for Indians and for everybody who actually experienced them, was of interest to him. It was of no interest whether or not Sitting Bull had really dreamed about the thunderbird; the Sioux uprising, the alliance with the Cheyenne and the defeat of Custer were of no interest. Crazy Horse and all the others, exile, imprisonment and the enigmatic sorrow you sensed in the misted eyes of Buffalo Bill himself were of no interest. The only thing that did interest little Elmer Dundy was hearing yet another story about the Wild West Show.

Later on, when he was grown man, he may have dreamed of Lahore, the Char Bagh in Delhi, the groves and the well-tended lawns of Lake Palace Hotel. He dreamed of the India of the maharajahs, the mist-shrouded oases between the Tigris and the Euphrates, far away from New York. And he translated it all into colonnaded pavilions, bridges, waterfalls, shell houses, follies, rock gardens, a decor of dreams and cardboard like the one he perhaps saw at the World's Columbian Exposition of 1893. And so, while Buffalo Bill continued on his long trek around the void, no longer drawing the same crowds as he once did, losing money, yet unable to stop, Elmer created Luna Park.

You reach it down a wide street, with a few cars here and there, between huge street lamps. And there are posters and billboards everywhere: *Capitol Luna*, and a large heart over the vast entrance with *"The Heart of Coney Island"* written inside it; and just underneath, in enormous letters: LUNA PARK, and then in small writing below that again: *Thompson & Dundy*.

At the entrance (price ten cents), the cashier keeps watch from a sort of boat-cum-counting-house. But inside, there's another whole city, with its street lamps, its leafy groves, its strange campaniles with coloured onion domes like Russian churches and folklore kremlins; its brass bands, its refreshment stands, its gently curving roofs, its pointed towers, its little painted houses, redolent of Prague and its castle, as much as of Italy, India or China. Because here, we're *any old where*. Crowds in boater hats stream past beneath plaster gargoyles, comic-book monsters, in a bargain-basement Venice. There's a mix of canals, fake castles, elephants with their African mahouts and their American flags. People squirt water, slither, slink, yell and punch each other. And then, at night, Luna Park sparkles, millions of little Tinker Bells settle on the roofs, the displays, the bridges, and along imaginary washing lines, like tiny stars fallen from the sky. And the sky is now less brilliant than the Earth. And the Earth has become the Moon, that old whatsit which used to make us dream, with the kind old face Plutarch talks about, its melancholy and its solitude.

But on the Moon in Luna Park, everything is spires, minarets and jollity. It's a break from the office and the factory floor. People jostle amiably, pleasantly bemused, and their eyes are turned towards the solitary heights of the towers, each of which strives to be the tallest. The days of Indians, bison, and all those cross-stitch panoramas of the Wild West are over. Audiences want something different now. That's what audiences are like. You have to keep inventing stuff for them. They want a show that's never been performed, a wild spectacle that doesn't yet exist. They want life itself. All of it. This is doubtless why Elmer Dundy keeps adding towers to Luna Park; it has to reach ever higher, shine ever brighter, and make one helluva racket!

But in the morning, when the sun comes up, the tat is obvious and the vulgarity is plain to see. The make-up has melted off. From his pilot's cabin, Elmer looks out at his sleeping forest, and he thinks back to the very first time he saw the Wild West Show. He feels a sort of nostalgia and something close to remorse. Spectacle, he says to himself, is definitely not what it used to be.

Finally, it's opening time. He looks down at the unseeing, indolent crowds as they enter his fiefdom. Master of Time and Solitude, Elmer has installed a small skylight in the narrow staircase that leads to human thought. And all he asks is that they glance through it, just for a moment, and take a look at his city of light, his paper angels, and that they believe— yes, that they make out they believe, just for a second—that it could be real. Elmer, like Buffalo Bill in the past, knows perfectly well that you let yourself be taken in—you marvel, you're hooked, you mount your wooden horse, you munch your waffle, and you shout "Ooh" and "Ah" as you ride the rollercoaster. Yet he also knows that these are not the Gardens of Paradise, but little pieces of iron piled up high to bring in serious money. Still, there's nothing to be despised about coming to douse your heart, amid the humid heat and the dead stones, with airy and terrifying sensations. It gives you a chance to meet someone, to place your hand on another hand, for a dress to lift a little and reveal a calf. People have a right to fall in love, he thinks, in the magnificent blaze of midnight, as they plunge into this poor man's abundance and leave their troubles behind. You've come by tram, the weather is fine, the sun beats down. You laugh amid this extraordinary thing which has been made *for us*. Oh! let the wheel rise and leave the two of us alone above the world. Everybody else looks so small, and suddenly our fatigue and our efforts are nothing; seen from here, our past life looks so tiny, but so beautiful! We don't know what to think. There's something frightening up here, when your seat on the Big Wheel leaves you suspended for a moment above the void. You look, and then everything is forgotten: the dust and the chaos, the money problems, having to make ends meet; there's just the glorious blue of New York Bay, the seagulls and the irrational feeling that sears us: "Is it possible that we're different? Different from the others? different from the people down there, now, queuing in the heat while we're up here, in the heavens?"

The Princes of Entertainment Die in Sorrow

ONCE THE WILD WEST SHOW had fulfilled its
civilizing mission and had profitably replaced the
Indians of Chateaubriand's day in people's minds—
because what people wanted was both the privileges
of the elect and the intoxication of the crowd, the mix
of old and new embodied by Buffalo Bill—and once
this mix had become both odious and indispensable,
each new generation suddenly thought it could read
the signs of an irreparable loss in its own nostalgia. And behind the walls of his small brick house,
between the old mahogany furniture and his print of
Naples, Buffalo Bill himself had sensed an indefin-
able debasement of reality.

As he trotted towards Madison Square on one
of his visits to New York, past the magnificent
foundations of Fifth Avenue, smiling or frowning
as he glanced in the shop windows, enjoying himself among the first devotees of shopping, but also

revolted by their invincible appetite, it suddenly became brutally apparent to Buffalo Bill that nostalgia wasn't just a vain resistance against the onslaught of novelty, but that it was now itself a form of knowledge. Civilization was this impossible blend of novelty and regret. And it was doubtless for this reason, and for no other, that Buffalo Bill Cody—who had inaugurated the new form that was mass entertainment—disappeared in turn into its grand oblivion.

Buffalo Bill, who had presented his staging of the entire world before Queen Victoria, who had even succeeded in captivating the austere William Gladstone; Buffalo Bill, who had had hundreds of horses gallop along moving pavements beneath the Eiffel Tower, and whose portrait had been pasted on every billboard on the planet; Buffalo Bill, who had even created a town that bore his birth name, Cody, and for whose benefit the Indians had sold their knick-knacks all the way from the Wild West to Russia; Buffalo Bill, who had raised his vast painted canvases before the world, and performed the drama of civilization to full houses, applauded by millions of spectators, and launched a veritable Americanomania, as his tasselled jackets and beaded braids sold like hot cakes; Buffalo Bill, who was the entrepreneur responsible for spectacles where the Indians never really died, but after rolling on the ground, stood up again when the shooting stopped, and quickly dusted down their jackets before launching themselves off afresh; Buffalo Bill, who had been seen with the same Indians taking gondola rides beneath the Rialto Bridge, and for whom the Colosseum had been judged too small, was beginning to grow old.

His routines are suddenly unsuited to the coming world. And, by the same process that relegated the Indians to imperceptibility, he in turn is slowly being drawn into the shadows. The clutch of words that he hurls at the spectators and the doffings of his Stetson no longer cut it. Buffalo Bill, who in France had been the model for the anonymous *gardian* in the Rhone delta—when, fascinated by the spectacle, which he saw in Arles, Baron Folco de Baroncelli-Javon kitted out his cowherds in costumes copied from the Wild West Show, thereby enabling the show to transmit its folklore to a real place, the Camargue (but who knows whether Greek theatre didn't inspire the dress of the hoplites of Sparta?); Buffalo Bill, whose circus animals are the ancestors of the herds of wild bison in Yellowstone Park; Buffalo Bill, whose face was at one time going to be carved on the National Memorial of the United States, which later became Mount Rushmore; Buffalo Bill, who had set the tone for a whole world, and who had set in motion the implacable commercial culture that will polish up a face, make it lovable and make it famous, before suddenly dropping it, was himself now beset by the void.

Very early on, right at the start of his career, Buffalo Bill had decided that each performance of the Show should begin in the following manner: a rider would do a lap of the arena brandishing the US flag, and then an orchestra of cowboys would play "The Star-Spangled Banner". The tune would later become the national anthem of the United States—and you can see how History bows down before spectacle. But that's not all. On one of his tours in England, the rider halted in front of the queen. Victoria rose to her feet and saluted the American flag. It was the first time that an English monarch had ever done such a thing. Which turns a two-bit circus act into a contribution to an unhoped-for diplomatic triumph.

*

All that's over now. The old ham is surrounded by his clapped-out wagons and his rusting rifles, exhausted, wrung out, always short of cash, with a knot in his stomach and sweating palms, suddenly gripped by real anxiety attacks. And, like all stars, having lived beyond his means, he's increasingly at the mercy of other people. Barnum's descendants have bought him out. But it's not enough; he'd borrowed too much. So, a huge tour is announced, a final Show. To clear his debts.

But all for nothing. Cinema is stealing the last of his spectators. Never mind! He can make films too! He tries his hand, but there are no audiences. His films are flops. Buffalo Bill has now played all his cards, and they're laid out on the table, greasy and dog-eared. His heart is no longer in it. His features are etched in every memory, but the caricature with a white horse and a white hat is all that remains of him. And now everything about him is white: his goatee beard, and even the hairs on his arse. The snow falls on Cody, warm and heavy. He's a grandfather. But he doesn't have time to take the air, or to sit his little grandchildren on his big dead knees. The old entertainer is skint, and he's also got debts;

he's washed-up and debt-ridden. In the films of his that have survived, you find him in grotesque pantomimes, making affected gestures. And when he performs alongside General Miles in a heavily edited version of the "Battle" of Wounded Knee—which is the name they've used again, one last time, for the massacre—they both appear on horseback, white-haired and several pounds heavier.

It's as a simple employee in the Sells-Floto Circus that he will end his spectacular career. The remains of his Show are sold off at auction, amid shreds of mist. At present, in return for a hundred dollars a day, he has to prance about on horseback, and, like Louis XIV in the past, he's—unfortunately—obliged to wear a wig so as to preserve his dignity intact and earn what it owes to the meanest part of creation. It's even written into his contract. So here he is, a pathetic figure but a touching sight, at the finishing post, stripped of the costume that previously sustained him, unwell and on the rubbish heap. Which is why the leader of the circus orchestra was moved by the sight of Bill Cody, glimpsed one evening through the open door of his dressing room, alone, still elegant for his age, a bald old clown obliged, even now, to make up and prepare for the umpteenth exhibition of his person. And we too are moved at the sight of this bogus dignity, the old actor gone to seed after years of life on the road, worn out and exiled in his dressing room. Buffalo Bill, the creator of the greatest sham of all time, suddenly finds that he belongs to a vanishing world and is instantly gripped by the great nostalgia.

In January 1917, less than two months after the last performance of his Show, an ageing William Cody—because he reverted to being William Cody and using his real name—paid a visit to his sister. Perhaps he began by navigating the foot of the Rockies for several hours in the cold dust. Then there were a few streaks of white in the sky, lightning ripped the horizon but not a drop of rain fell. Suddenly, there was a violent storm; his white horse tacked into the wind, nervous, and lost in the mist. But on the eighth day of January, he sighted land. Struck by the beauty of the place, like one of those tiny creatures that crawl towards the light, he hugged the last coastline of his life, berthed, and then, when his lungs became excessively inflamed after catching a chill, he fell seriously ill.

Through his bedroom window he could see the vast spectacle of things. From time to time he would still adopt a stage voice, a tone in which to harangue the world, and then he would exhibit the forced jollity of a worthless bum. He made an effort to laugh, but his secret wound hadn't healed, and the ceiling reflected back to him the worst pangs in his heart. What had he done? His face was pale, his skull gleamed. Oh! reality was terrible with a cold food tray beside the bed, a lukewarm glass of water and a pillow that felt too hot and was soaked in sweat.

Cody became sentimental. He wept at the least thing, held his sister's hand squeezed tight in his own and sighed. Like an old plant, he wished he could produce one more flower and smell its perfume! But Cody was already dead, and had been for a long time. In becoming Buffalo Bill, he had disappeared behind the tasselled jackets and the bravura repartee. Yes, Cody was dead, but not like Sitting Bull; his quintessential being had transmogrified into America itself. A living legend is a dead person. And now, seventy million spectators later, he needed to be resurrected in order to become a living being as he entered the gates of death for real. And this he could not do. He

continued to perform, hamming it up to the last.
There is nothing finer than spectacle.

One morning, William Cody's voice turned reedy.
His belly swelled. He didn't even look towards the
window. He could feel the exhausted wellspring
inside him, the ice, the incurable wound; time
slipped its long skeleton fingers beneath his skin. For
a moment, perhaps, he saw a cotton dress, beautiful
children, a landscape. And then it was like a rush-
ing stream through his flesh, a deluge. And, in a last
burst of consciousness, he saw how far he would have
to climb in order to live another life... And then, it
seemed to him that life had been a horrible trap. An
hour passed. Sunlight entered the room. His breath-
ing was a little easier. And all at once he thought he
saw his mistakes so clearly that he loved them. He
felt his back slide slowly against the rough sheet,
tiny clusters of dust particles swirled by his bed,
and he saw a wide plain, with bodies lying on it, and
the snow that served as their shroud; he opened his
mouth, but he no longer had the strength to speak.
He couldn't say anything. Ah! he suddenly had so
much to recount... so many details, and so many

secrets to tell. He closed his eyes. We'll never know. We're born never to know. We'll have had fifteen or thirty years, and all the time we'll have been alone, in the company of other people, and we'll have loved them very powerfully, but *sotto voce*. No one has ever been a child, not a single soul. We've never been anything other than blind and deaf.

The morning was already well advanced. The sun had warmed the pillow and, when he slowly turned his head, he felt the warmth of the sheet on his cheek. Lord, it felt good! Shouldn't that have been enough? Everything was so distant now... What had happened? All he hoped was that his sister would come upstairs this morning; he would so much have liked her to be with him, for a moment. He didn't want to die alone, crammed inside his wound. Ah! if only someone could have been there, beside him. He wanted to die like everyone else.

But death is patient. It stands facing the bed, like a spectator in front of the stage. There's no escaping it. It's paid for its seat, and it will see us croak.

Histories

AFTER THE MASSACRE OF WOUNDED KNEE, the Indians eked out a miserable existence on uncultivated and divided territories. Those who had worked for the Wild West Show returned after a few years, but their luck didn't improve. The Redskins were viewed as the remnants of an old world, and the watchword was now *assimilation*.

The destruction of a people always happens by degrees, and each phase, in its own way, is innocent of the preceding one. The spectacle that seized upon the Indians in the final moments of their history was not the least of the violence perpetrated against them. It casts our original consent into oblivion. In every case, the initial infatuation lasted no more than an instant. Then, each time, there followed the same uncontainable destruction. And no world of words was ever able to generate its world of things.

SO NOW LET'S LOOK. Yes, let's look very hard, with all our might. Let's look at them, from the vantage point of our outrageous ease and prodigality.

And then let's imagine for a moment—oh, just a brief moment—that everything we have around us, our houses, our furniture, our kit, even our names, our memories, and then our friends, our jobs, everything, absolutely everything could be taken away from us, jeered and confiscated. "Oh, of course," we say, "Yes, yes, we've thought about it", and "Obviously we knew about it." But it's all abstract, just words, a hypothesis. Yes, it's a hypothesis. Other people. A hypothesis. Well, let's try harder, just a little bit harder, to see if we can deduce anything from it. Let's try telling ourselves, now, that this hypothesis has been going on for a very long time, in fact, my God, it's been going on forever.

And the people in this photograph no longer have a home, and most of their memories are gone. For them, it's not just a hypothesis. Look more closely.

Yes, you know them, in fact, you know them very well, you've seen them a hundred times, two hundred times. Oh of course, they're not exactly the same, not exactly the same as these people, and yet, if you look carefully, you've seen them before.

Let's take another look. You don't just feel a strange unease at the sight of their destitution, you also feel a sort of sympathy. Yes, don't let's be afraid of words: we feel sympathy. It's existed since the dawn of time, but where, in God's name, does this sympathy come from? No one knows. It's something that courses through your body, your eyes, it takes you by the throat and fills your breast with tears. It's a strange phenomenon, sympathy. We must be a little bit like these poor wretches. Because poor wretches is what they are, always the same frail figures, the same cluster of children, the same rags.

Yes, let's take another look at them, at the time when their history is coming to an end, and ours is beginning. Ah! it's both moving and painful to look at them. And if we find it painful, if we feel a dull angst, it's because, despite the smile we detect on the man's face, we know, yes, we know very well, that they're going to die. And because they're going to die, and we know it, sensing it without seeing it, we suddenly feel very close to them, *like them*; except that *we* are not actually dying; *we* hardly ever die.

Let's look at them: they're the survivors of Wounded Knee. They must be in some sort of camp, a few days after the massacre, a few hours before the grand spectacle takes hold of them and delivers them up to us. And they look at us: the women, the children and the fellow on the right with his funny fur hat, his sad smile, his sorrowful eyes and his US Army jacket snatched, perhaps by an irony of fate, out of the need to clothe himself.

A photograph is a peculiar thing. Truth lives within it as if it were inseparable from its sign. And, all of a sudden, I seem to see not just these poor wretches, but the very incarnation of poverty—as if this testimony exceeded its occasion. And I say to myself: these are Big Foot's Miniconjou, and will be until the end of time, they're the performers in the Wild West Show, they're poor devils, and they belong to the same family as the people who hold out their hand to us, anywhere we find ourselves, outside the cathedral or McDonald's. Yes, it's still the same fellow and the same few women sitting on the ground with the ugly face of poverty.

May the fellow from Dakota forgive us, and, if he can, return from his past narrative tense with his beggar's pouch of worries, where shards of History lock together like jaws. Let's take one last look.

Let us love his sorrow; we share his incomprehension, his children are our own, his funny hat might suit us! Let's take a good look at him. It's a sleepless night. Whisper to me what I must write. But please, don't show me your face any more, don't look at me. The earth sorrows, the body is alone. I can't see anything now. And there you are, a destitute king because you picked the wrong card.

Snow

SNOW IS THE MOST BEAUTIFUL THING in the world. A snowflake is a cluster of crystals, like a diamond, but diamond is one of the hardest materials found on the planet. Hercules's helmet, Kronos's scythe and Prometheus's chains were all hewn from diamond. A snowflake, by contrast, is extremely fragile.

There's nothing more fragile or more beautiful than a snowflake. Like all creatures, it exists in multiple forms. And so, while the Wild West Show was touring the world and reaching the peak of its fame, and while the last of the Indian tribes, now decimated, were being herded into overcrowded reserves, Wilson Alwyn Bentley was growing up quietly in Jericho, Vermont. As a teenager he roamed the countryside, climbed the hills and moseyed about among the maples. He thinks he can read tree bark. As he listens to the buzzing of flies, he can hear talk. When

winter comes, he spends all his time outside; as soon
as he gets in from school, and has eaten a good slice
of pie, he's off trekking, like all Yankees in Vermont.
But he never goes very far, he slashes along the paths
that take him to the immensity of tiny things. His
mother is a schoolteacher. She bought him an old
microscope, and every day he takes it out of its pretty
pyramid-base box. He sets it up, slides open the tray
and places a glass-and-bone plate on the flat surface.
Very delicately, the tweezers tear a scrap of snow
from the window ledge. It's there on the plate. Little
Wilson bends over the lens, and he can see. Wilson,
the farmer's son, the yokel from Vermont, can see.
The white stub slowly melts on its glass plate. Wilson
looks as long as he can. He's fifteen years old.

For five years, he observes everything nature offers
him: pine-cone scales, acorns, leaves, seeds, pebbles,
petals, feathers, everything. Wilson wants to see it
all. He's drawn to anything small, as if the world were
more beautiful in that form, humbler, more delicate,
but also more abundant, stranger, and also vaster,
as if there were some kind of sorcery in the imperceptible, and as if another world, at once minuscule
but in reality vast, mind-bogglingly enormous, were

hidden there on a different scale. It makes Wilson feel giddy. No one snowflake is like another. To begin with, he thought he'd found a single design; but he was wrong. God has created as many designs as there are snowflakes. And so as not to lose this marvellous beauty, Wilson draws them. But the snowflakes disappear. Pfft! He never has time to finish his drawing. His own breath melts the flakes. It's as if God wanted to preserve the secret of their infinite individuality.

When he's around seventeen, his parents finally buy him a camera. He secures the camera to the microscope, and sets it up outside. The snowflakes fall on the plate, the weather is cold. Willie's shaking hands turn the focusing wheel. Holding his breath, he presses the button, and Pop! the snowflake has been captured by the silver spangles. But the images remain blurred. From time to time he loses heart. "Hast thou entered into the treasures of the snow?" God asks a recalcitrant Job; and Willie tells himself that God doesn't want photography to penetrate matter, that its mystery will not allow itself to be pierced. For a year, he keeps trying, refuses to give up. And at last he succeeds in photographing a snowflake, the first that anyone has ever captured.

So he embarks on a tremendous pursuit, a pursuit that's at once tiny and tremendous. He photographs hundreds of snowflakes. It's a miracle. There are no two alike. And while Buffalo Bill goes from town to town, doffing his Stetson tens and hundreds of times over, in a rumble of applause, Wilson is discovering the infinite variety behind what he thought was the same. He is discovering that, if you hold your breath for a moment and hunker down in the heart of your impressions, things that at first glance appear identical or imperceptible, will, when seen from very close, as the wind whips and the cold bites, subsequently separate out, and become particular, distinct. And you no longer know whether anything you could call snow, or snowflakes, actually exists, because they're all different, all equal but dissimilar, strangely singular.

Nature is a spectacle. Oh, of course it's not the only one. There's thought. And others too. And Wilson, the crackpot from Vermont, can suddenly see that life is all disparity, that whether it's snowflakes or marks made by your ball on the wall in the yard, no two are the same. And now he starts to examine drops of water, steam, mist—all those tiny, unpredictable, imponderable phenomena. A drop of water is such an extraordinary thing, with its deceiving transparency, its curves, its bulge, its incredible reflections. Wilson is flabbergasted. He's stunned by all these hidden riches. And he doesn't understand why people don't look more carefully, why people don't examine pine cones more closely, or tree bark, and pebbles from the river. He's fascinated by lightness. Disarmed by inconsistency. Enchanted by softness.

And while Americans become ever more frantic, and people rush to all four corners of the continent to grub around in the earth, foul up the cracks in its surface, start banks, show off their legs and come up against their desires like stone hurdles, Wilson remains quietly in Vermont, on his parents' farm. Looking. This is all he does. And he takes hundreds of photographs of pine-cone scales, moss filaments, flower petals, snail shells, lichen; he's interested in dwarf forms, in things that are diminutive, or stunted. But what amazes him the most, dumbfounds and mesmerizes him, are things that melt, or flow, or stream, or burn, or thaw, or fade, or hide, or disappear. The things he finds the most beautiful, the most enthralling, are things that you can't look at for long, which don't recur, which only happen once, just once—there, right in front of you—and which last no longer than an instant. And then vanish. This is what intrigues him. He wishes he didn't have to miss any of them. He'd like to capture them all, to preserve something from them, an imprint, a trace, a memento.

Oh, Wilson Bentley must be a bit cracked. Yes, he's quite possibly a bit cracked. He spends hours alone, lying on a trellis, between the imperceptible tinkle of snowflakes on a glass plate and some unheard cry deep inside him. And if he loves photographing scales, feathers and seeds, he has a real weakness for snow. For snow is both soft and cold, beautiful and terrifyingly imperious towards humans. It blankets everything. Snow lies there, motionless, tenacious, enveloping the world, dazzling and monotonous.

And what Wilson fears the most would be to miss a snowflake, a single snowflake, to fail to capture each of its dancing, airborne, celestial and almost immaterial particles. He has the impression, as he lies on his trellis in the yard behind the farm, that, with his tweezers, he can physically touch the suprasensible. No sooner has he bent over the tiny crystal, the one just fallen from the sky, the tiny fragment of meteor, than it vanishes. You have to act quickly. Very quickly. If you want to etch this unique existence onto your photographic plate, the imprint which will be its grave, or, in a sense, its tome, like a fleeting sensation that you want to fix, you have to be lying in wait, at the ready, alert, responsive. In the few photographs that I've seen of him, Wilson is in the snow, outside his farm, photographing a snowflake, and smiling.

Without his having intended it, his pictures became famous, and were known throughout the world. He published some magnificent photographs in the *National Geographic* under the heading: "The Magic Beauty of Snow and Dew". He describes the masterpieces of nature which carelessly deposits the shapes of trees, ferns, coral and lace on our bedroom windows.

It's said that he played the clarinet and imitated the sound of birds, turkeys and frogs. This may be true. His imagination is indisputable, but people must have made some of it up. He photographed the smile of young girls, but not one of these photographs has survived. He noted down everything: the weather, the clothes he wore, the day's news items, how many litres of milk his farm had sold, everything and nothing. For him, the smallest details had their importance. But the essential part of his life was concentrated in his eyes. Wilson existed entirely in his eyes, as if living consisted in seeing, looking, as if he were haunted by the visible world, as if he were desperately searching for something. But what? Nothing perhaps. Just the sense of time perishing, forms failing.

As he grew older, he attempted the impossible: he wanted to photograph the wind. But photography kills everything it captures, movement dies in its slide holders. Even cinema can't do it. You can only film the effects of wind, not the wind itself. He tried. I've never seen his photographs of breeze and blizzards; and I have no wish to see them. I can imagine them. A little later on, he also photographed drops of dew. It's said that he looked out for them in the morning on the legs of grasshoppers.

He was an inveterate storyteller, stuck Chinese lanterns on the ceiling, played croquet in the dining room and shared scraps of his whimsical, upbeat philosophy with children. He loved the cinema. A fan of Mary Pickford, he never missed a film of hers, and would play the organ during the interval. When he fell in love with a schoolteacher, Mina Seeley, he was apparently content just to scratch her initials on a windowpane with his finger. Which is not inconsiderable.

He sold his prints for five cents apiece, and then the patterns turned up replicated on extremely expensive jewellery in Tiffany's. He never knew either wealth or fame. After his parents died, he lived alone in a small part of their house, while his brothers and sisters occupied the rest. One fine day, at the age of sixty-six, as he was out walking in the snow, ten kilometres away from home, the cold got to his bones; but he still wanted—absolutely—to see something, a beautiful ice stalactite hanging from a pine branch. A storm blew up. People called him. But he went on looking. He looked at the delicate, graceful shape of the piece of ice, its slender, fragile, sensitive stem, its vaporous fringe. He was carried home unconscious. It was Christmas Eve. On the day he was buried, it's said that it snowed.

PHOTOGRAPH CREDITS

p. 24: *Sitting Bull and Buffalo Bill, Montreal, QC, 1885,* Wm. Notman & Son, 1885, nineteenth century II-83126 © McCord Museum

p. 62, 76: © National Anthropological Archives, Smithsonian

p. 114: © Library of Congress, Prints & Photographs Division, Detroit Publishing Company Collection, [LC-DIG-det-4a11115 (digital file from original)]

p. 143 (and 144): © Library of Congress, Prints & Photographs Division, John C.H. Grabill Collection, [LC-DIG-ppmsc-02517 (digital file from original print)]

p. 148: © W. Bentley, Buffalo Museum of Science

IN THE BEGINNING WAS THE SEA
TOMÁS GONZÁLEZ

'Smoothly intriguing narrative, with its touches of sinister, Patricia Highsmith-like menace' *Irish Times*

BEWARE OF PITY
STEFAN ZWEIG

'Zweig's fictional masterpiece' *Guardian*

THE ENCOUNTER
PETRU POPESCU

'A book that suggests new ways of looking at the world and our place within it' *Sunday Telegraph*

WAKE UP, SIR!
JONATHAN AMES

'The novel is extremely funny but it is also sad and poignant, and almost incredibly clever' *Guardian*

THE WORLD OF YESTERDAY
STEFAN ZWEIG

'*The World of Yesterday* is one of the greatest memoirs of the twentieth century, as perfect in its evocation of the world Zweig loved, as it is in its portrayal of how that world was destroyed' David Hare

WAKING LIONS
AYELET GUNDAR-GOSHEN

'A literary thriller that is used as a vehicle to explore big moral issues. I loved everything about it' *Daily Mail*

BONITA AVENUE
PETER BUWALDA

'One wild ride: a swirling helix of a family saga... a new writer as toe-curling as early Roth, as roomy as Franzen and as caustic as Houellebecq' *Sunday Telegraph*

JOURNEY BY MOONLIGHT
ANTAL SZERB

'Just divine... makes you imagine the author has had private access to your own soul' Nicholas Lezard, *Guardian*